Presented to:

_____

From:

_____

Date:

_____

MEN'S DEVOTIONAL BIBLE
DAILY DEVOTIONS FROM GODLY MEN
Copyright © 1993 by The Zondervan Corporation

ISBN 0-310-96204-8

Request for information should be addressed to:
Zondervan Publishing House,
5300 Patterson Ave., S.E.,
Grand Rapids, Michigan 49530

Project Editor: Martha Manikas-Foster

Printed in Hong Kong

95 96 /❖ HK / 7 6

January 1

Then God said, "Let us make man in our image, in our likeness, and let them rule over the fish of the sea and the birds of the air, over the livestock, over all the earth, and over all the creatures that move along the ground."
Genesis 1:26

Passage for the Day: Genesis 1:26–31

As a human created in God's image, you are inherently significant and when you work you are doing something that is very Godlike. It is not only God's work that is significant; human work is significant, too. It is something ordained by God. The fact that you work is, in the words of Genesis 1, "very good." Intrinsically good. Valued by God.

— **Doug Sherman and William Hendricks**

January 2

*"You are the light of the world.
A city on a hill cannot be hidden."
Matthew 5:14*

Passage for the Day: Matthew 5:14–16

If we are called by God to holiness of life and if holiness is beyond our natural power to achieve (which it certainly is) then it follows that God himself must give us the light, the strength and the courage to fulfill the task he requires of us. He will certainly give us the grace we need. If we do not become saints it is because we do not avail ourselves of his gift.

— Thomas Merton

January 3

For you, O God, tested us;
you refined us like silver.
Psalm 66:10

Passage for the Day: Psalm 66:8–12

There would be other difficulties in my life but none as difficult or scary as almost losing my wife. I still had a lot to learn about priorities and my faith and my ego, but I could never again say that God hadn't led me through some deep waters to strengthen me for when those new lessons came.

— Joe Gibbs

*The body is a unit, though it is made up
of many parts; and though all its parts are many,
they form one body. So it is with Christ.*
1 Corinthians 12:12

Passage for the Day: 1 Corinthians 12:12–31

If all cells [in one's body] were the same, where would the body be? As it is, there are many cells, but one body.

That analogy conveys a more precise meaning to me because though a hand or foot or ear cannot have a life separate from the body, a cell does have that potential. . . . Some cells do choose to live in the body; sharing its benefits while maintaining complete independence—they become parasites or cancer cells.

— **Paul Brand**

January 5

*"But you must not eat from the tree
of the knowledge of good and evil,
for when you eat of it you will surely die."*
Genesis 2:17

Passage for the Day: Genesis 2:15–17

Free will, though it makes evil possible, is also the only thing that makes possible any love or goodness or joy worth having. . . . The happiness which God designs for his higher creatures is the happiness of being freely, voluntarily united to him and to each other in an ecstasy of love and delight compared with which the most rapturous love between a man and woman on this earth is mere milk and water. And for that they must be free.

— C.S. Lewis

January 6

*"Your kingdom come, your will be done
on earth as it is in heaven."*
Matthew 6:10

Passage for the Day: Matthew 6:5–15

[In Matthew 6:10, Jesus] was telling us to embark upon a most tragic search for the will of God in our lives. Try as I might, I cannot find any place to hide in those crystal, bleeding sentences. Human words find it hard to express the depth of Jesus' divine words. But he was saying, in the most literal way, that God's will should be sought and it should be obeyed.

— Jack Perry

January 7

Let us then approach the throne of grace
with confidence, so that we may receive mercy
and find grace to help us in our time of need.
Hebrews 4:16

Passage for the Day: Hebrews 4:14–16

We are not second-class citizens. The Bible says we are part of God's family. Hebrews 4 records that Jesus, who is now in heaven, intercedes for us and that he understands our weaknesses.

— Jim Conway

January 8

And after he became the father of Methuselah,
Enoch walked with God 300 years and
had other sons and daughters.
Genesis 5:22

Passage for the Day: Genesis 5:21–24

Enoch walked with God; he enjoyed a relationship with God; and he pleased God. We could accurately say he was devoted to God. This is the meaning of godliness.

— Jerry Bridges

January 9

"Therefore everyone who hears these words of mine and puts them into practice is like a wise man who built his house on the rock."
Matthew 7:24

Passage for the Day: Matthew 7:24–27

All my life I had made my football career the number-one priority and let it dictate the direction of my life. Now here was the Bible saying I needed to make God and his will first and follow his direction for my life. . . . What my new Christian experience did do for me was to place football behind the priorities of my faith and my family and give me a sense of confidence and peace about the future—whatever it would be.

— **Tom Landry**

January 10

We will not hide them from their children;
we will tell the next generation the
praiseworthy deeds of the LORD,
his power, and the wonders he has done.
Psalm 78:4

Passage for the Day: Psalm 78:1–8

According to the Christian values that govern my life, my most important reason for living is to get . . . the gospel safely in the hands of my children. Of course, I want to place it in as many other hands as possible; *nevertheless, my number one responsibility is to evangelize my own children.* I hope millions of other fathers agree with that ultimate priority.

— **James Dobson**

January 11

*But thanks be to God! He gives us the victory
through our Lord Jesus Christ.*
1 Corinthians 15:57

Passage for the Day: 1 Corinthians 15:51–58

Dear Father, my death and the deaths of people I love are a mystery. Although I may not give up searching out the mystery, I do not want to torture myself to know the unknowable. You have penetrated and conquered it. My hope is in you; I need no more. Your saving grace is enough. Thank you, through Christ my Lord. Amen.

— **Philip W. Williams**

January 12

*So Sarah laughed to herself as she thought,
"After I am worn out and my master is old, will
I now have this pleasure?"
Genesis 18:12*

Passage for the Day: Genesis 18:9–15

When Abram is pushing a century of years and Sarai ninety . . . God pays them a visit and tells them they had better select a name for their new son [see Genesis 17:17–19]. . . . They laugh because that is what you do when someone says he can do the impossible. They laugh a little *at* God, and a lot *with* God—for God is laughing, too. Then, with the smile still on his face, he gets busy doing what he does best—the unbelievable.

— Max Lucado

January 13

*Jesus replied, "Foxes have holes and birds of the air
have nests, but the Son of Man has
no place to lay his head."*
Matthew 8:20

Passage for the Day: Matthew 8:18–22

Time after time I find that men and women in the prisons of America want nothing to do with the church. . . . But I see those same people come alive when I talk about Jesus the prisoner, the outcast who was followed by a dirty dozen, the One who was laid in a borrowed manger, rode on a borrowed donkey, was arrested, hung on a cross between two thieves, and then buried in a borrowed tomb. They can understand and identify with the Jesus of the Scriptures, not with a Christ who appears to have just stepped out of a Brooks Brothers catalog.

— **Charles Colson**

Better is one day in your courts than a thousand elsewhere; I would rather be a doorkeeper in the house of my God than dwell in the tents of the wicked.
Psalm 84:10

Passage for the Day: Psalm 84:8–12

In verse 11 we learn the reason for such devotion. The Lord is pictured as a "sun and shield." He offers warmth, blessing, protection and prosperity. He does not withhold anything good from those whose walk with him is blameless. . . . O Lord, today I rededicate my life to your service. Be my sun and shield, and give me the satisfaction of knowing that my walk is worthy of my calling.

— Don Wyrtzen

January 15

Do not show partiality in judging; hear both small and great alike. Do not be afraid of any man, for judgment belongs to God. Bring me any case too hard for you, and I will hear it.
Deuteronomy 1:17

Passage for the Day: Deuteronomy 1:15–18

Being nice translates to accepting each person for his or her individual worth. It disturbs me that some still decide that certain people are not worth bothering with simply because of their socio-economic class, job title or national origin. *Everyone has value.*
— **Ben Carson**

January 16

*Early the next morning Abraham got up
and saddled his donkey. He took with him two
of his servants and his son Isaac.
When he had cut enough wood for the burnt offering,
he set out for the place God had told him about.
Genesis 22:3*

Passage for the Day: Genesis 22:1–14

Sacrifice in the Bible means that we give to God the best we have; it is the finest form of worship. Sacrifice is not giving up things, but giving to God with joy the best we have.

— **Oswald Chambers**

ACKNOWLEDGMENTS

Dan B. Allender: Selections used for May 17 and June 7. Taken from THE WOUNDED HEART by Dan Allender. Copyright © 1990 by Dan B. Allender. Used by permission of NavPress.

John B. Anderson: Selections used for June 20 and September 3. Taken from BETWEEN TWO WORLDS by John B. Anderson. Copyright © 1970 by Zondervan Publishing House. Used by permission.

Stephen Arterburn: Selections used for February 2, April 7, July 12, October 12, and November 14. Taken from THE ANGRY MAN by Stephen Arterburn and David Stoop. Copyright © 1991 by Stephen Arterburn and David Stoop. Used by permission of Word, Inc., Dallas, Texas.

David Atkinson: Selection used for April 2. Taken from THE MESSAGE OF RUTH by David Atkinson. Copyright © 1983 by David Atkinson. Used by permission of InterVarsity Press, P.O. Box 1400, Downers Grove, IL 60515.

David Augsburger: Selections used for April 20 and June 4. Taken from CHERISHABLE: LOVE AND MARRIAGE by David Augsburger. Copyright © 1971 by Herald Press. Used by permission.

Joseph Bayly: Selection used for September 12. Taken from PSALMS OF MY LIFE by Joseph Bayly, available at your local Christian bookstore. Copyright © 1987 by the estate of Joseph Bayly. Used by permission of David C. Cook Publishing Co.

Bob Benson: Selections used for September 22, October 2, November 2, November 17, December 1, and December 10. Taken from "SEE YOU AT THE HOUSE" by Bob Benson. Copyright © 1989 by Generoux Nelson, a division of Thomas Nelson Publishers. Used by permission.

Donald Bloesch: Selections used for February 23, August 17, and September 28. Taken from THE STRUGGLE OF PRAYER by Donald G. Bloesch. Copyright © 1980 by Donald G. Bloesch. Used by permission of HarperCollins Publishers.

January 17

"For my yoke is easy and my burden is light."
Matthew 11:30

Passage for the Day: Matthew 11:28–30

Only the man who follows the command of Jesus single-mindedly, and unresistingly lets his yoke rest upon him, finds his burden easy, and under its gentle pressure receives the power to persevere in the right way. The command of Jesus is hard, unutterably hard, for those who try to resist it. But for those who willingly submit, the yoke is easy and the burden is light.

— **Dietrich Bonhoeffer**

December 31

*For the message of the cross is foolishness
to those who are perishing, but to us who
are being saved it is the power of God.
1 Corinthians 1:18*

Passage for the Day: 1 Corinthians 1:18–31

The message is gripping: Show a man his failures without Jesus, and the result will be found in the roadside gutter. Give a man religion without reminding him of his filth, and the result will be arrogance in a three-piece suit. But get the two in the same heart—get sin to meet Savior and Savior to meet sin—and the result just might be another Pharisee turned preacher who sets the world on fire.

— Max Lucado

January 18

May the favor of the Lord our God rest upon us;
establish the work of our hands for us—yes,
establish the work of our hands.
Psalm 90:17

Passage for the Day: Psalm 90:13–17

Christianity . . . has always provided a connection between work and worship. Men can dignify labor by doing ordinary things, but as redeemed persons. There lies the difference, and this is where the drudgery dissipates—God is in it. That means that every work bench in a plant is an altar! . . . So you see, we can please the Lord by our work.

— **Ted Engstrom and**
David Juroe

December 30

"But let him who boasts boast about this:
that he understands and knows me, that I am the LORD,
who exercises kindness, justice and righteousness on
earth, for in these I delight," declares the LORD.
Jeremiah 9:24

Passage for the Day: Jeremiah 9:23–24

If you're a dad, what kind of mark are you leaving on your children, especially your sons? Do you realize that your little boys are watching you like hawks? They're trying to figure out what maleness is all about, and you're their model. I hope they see in you a deep, uncompromising love for God.

— **Bill Hybels**

January 19

Indeed, in our hearts we felt the sentence of death.
But this happened that we might not rely
on ourselves but on God, who raises the dead.
2 Corinthians 1:9

Passage for the Day: 2 Corinthians 1:8–11

God, who has made us, knows what we are and that our happiness lies in him. Yet we will not seek it in him as long as he leaves us any other resort where it can even plausibly be looked for. While what we call "our own life" remains agreeable we will not surrender it to him.

— **C.S. Lewis**

December 29

Therefore go and make disciples of all nations,
baptizing them in the name of the Father
and of the Son and of the Holy Spirit.
Matthew 28:19

Passage for the Day: Matthew 28:16–20

I have learned that when God looks upon his Body, spread like an archipelago throughout the world, he sees the whole thing. And I think he, understanding the cultural backgrounds and true intent of the worshipers, likes the variety he sees.

— **Paul Brand**

January 20

And God said to him, "I am God Almighty;
be fruitful and increase in number.
A nation and a community of nations will come
from you, and kings will come from your body."
Genesis 35:11

Passage for the Day: Genesis 35:9–13

In giving life and love to a child, whether by birth or by adoption, we participate most nearly in what it means to be made in God's image because then we share—if only to a limited degree—the chiefest attributes of God the Father himself. Not to offer love to our own children is to miss one of the foretastes of eternity, the grace of posterity as a sacrament of everlasting life.

— **D. Bruce Lockerbie**

December 28

The righteous care about justice for the poor,
but the wicked have no such concern.
Proverbs 29:7

Passage for the Day: Proverbs 29:1–7

The Christian is committed to work for justice and
righteousness, to bring the gospel of Christ to bear in all areas of life
to make a difference in society. But we do it by the integrity of our
witness, not be resorting to quick, simplistic clichés.

— **Charles Colson**

January 21

Wives, submit to your husbands as to the Lord.
Ephesians 5:22

Passage for the Day: Ephesians 5:21–33

If a man exercised his authority in the way it is outlined in the Bible, a woman would not resent it. She would find herself served. She would find her needs met. She would have her say, be able to exercise her gifts, not be pushed back and ignored and treated like a second-class citizen. God's design for marriage is for husbands to love their wives as Christ loved the church and for wives to respect their husbands. Christ loved the church enough to die for it, and that kind of love is worthy of respect.

— **Mike Singletary**

December 27

*Rather, we have renounced secret and shameful ways;
we do not use deception, nor do we distort the
word of God. On the contrary, by setting forth the
truth plainly we commend ourselves to
every man's conscience in the sight of God.*
2 Corinthians 4:2

Passage for the Day: 2 Corinthians 4:1–6

The rule is this: Christians are people who remember their
own weaknesses and failure. They are under reconstruction. So they
offer hope and forgiveness to people who fall and who need Jesus'
healing grace and hope.

— **Donald M. Joy**

January 22

For he will command his angels concerning you
to guard you in all your ways.
Psalm 91:11

Passage for the Day: Psalm 91:9–16

Believers, look up—take courage. The angels are nearer than you think.

— Billy Graham

December 26

Therefore I will give him a portion among the great, and he will divide the spoils with the strong, because he poured out his life unto death, and was numbered with the transgressors. For he bore the sin of many, and made intercession for the transgressors.
Isaiah 53:12

Passage for the Day: Isaiah 53:1–12

If we are to know [God], we must know him as he is: our perfect, all-knowing God who sacrificed himself for us when we were helpless. He gave up, not just his glory to become man, but his own life—the just for the unjust, the deserving for the undeserving. His initiative broke the barrier.

— **Tim Stafford**

January 23

Therefore, if anyone is in Christ, he is a new creation;
the old has gone, the new has come!
2 Corinthians 5:17

Passage for the Day: 2 Corinthians 5:16–21

[The] unfathomable idea of an actual identity exchange is implicit in conversion. . . . As a result of this stuff-exchange, we carry within us not just the image of, or the philosophy of, or faith in, but the actual substance of God. One staggering consequence credits us with the spiritual genes of Christ; as we stand before God, we are judged on the basis of Christ's perfection, not our own unworthiness.

— Paul Brand

December 25

They said to the woman,
"We no longer believe just because of what you said;
now we have heard ourselves, and we know
that this man really is the Savior of the world."
John 4:42

Passage for the Day: John 4:39–42

If Christmas means anything to you, then it must mean everything. It is a beginning and an end. It is a time of darkness and inexpressible light. . . . Celebrate . . . most heartily, amidst the dung of the stable, which is, of course, the refuse of the world. Celebrate at the foot of that ghastly cross because it is the hope of the world. Gather around a cattle trough and celebrate a baby born in poverty and rejected, because he is the Savior of the world!

— **Michael Card**

January 24

Meanwhile, the Midianites sold Joseph in Egypt
to Potiphar, one of Pharaoh's officials,
the captain of the guard.
Genesis 37:36

Passage for the Day: Genesis 37:1–36

Through all his trials, Joseph learned to trust: not that God
would prevent hardship, but that he would redeem even the
hardship. Choking back tears, Joseph tried to explain his faith to his
murderous brothers: "You intended to harm me, but God intended it
for good" (Genesis 50:20).

— **Philip Yancey**

December 24

And there were shepherds living out in the fields nearby,
keeping watch over their flocks at night.
Luke 2:8

Passage for the Day: Luke 2:8–15

The announcement went first to the shepherds. . . . Men who didn't have a reputation to protect or an ax to grind or a ladder to climb. Men who didn't know enough to tell God that angels don't sing to sheep and that messiahs aren't found wrapped in rags and sleeping in a feed trough. . . .

So . . .
while the theologians were sleeping
and the elite were dreaming
and the successful were snoring
the meek were kneeling.
They were kneeling before the One only the meek will see.

— Max Lucado

January 25

*He replied, "Because you have so little faith. I tell you
the truth, if you have faith as small as a mustard seed,
you can say to this mountain, 'Move from here to there'
and it will move. Nothing will be impossible for you."*
Matthew 17:20

Passage for the Day: Matthew 17:14–23

The giver of this grain of faith is God, whose Son, though
despondent and despairing in his crisis, maintained his faith. He
went through his Gethsemane of grief with the word "Father" still
on his lips.

— **Philip W. Williams**

December 23

But after he had considered this, an angel of the Lord
appeared to him in a dream and said,
"Joseph son of David, do not be afraid to take Mary
home as your wife, because what is conceived
in her is from the Holy Spirit."
Matthew 1:20

Passage for the Day: Matthew 1:18–25

We know almost nothing about Joseph, apart from his gentleness and willingness to say "No" to himself for Mary's sake and for God's. . . .We know for certain that Jesus made it to manhood with a wonderfully strong and simple version of what *father* meant. He must have learned it at least in part from Joseph. Before he shrieked, "Abba!" with a man's tormented voice in the garden of Gethsemane, he must have tenderly called out that same name in an innocent child's voice to that man in the shadows, Joseph.

— **Michael Card**

January 26

As for man, his days are like grass, he flourishes like a flower of the field; the wind blows over it and it is gone, and its place remembers it no more.
Psalm 103:15

Passage for the Day: Psalm 103:1–22

I'm suggesting that we stop and consider the brevity of our years on earth, perhaps finding new motivation to preserve the values that will endure. Why should we work ourselves into an early grave, missing those precious moments with loved ones who crave our affection and attention? It is a question that every man and woman should consider.

Let me offer this final word of encouragement for those who are determined to slow the pace: once you get out from under constant pressure, you'll wonder why you drove yourself so hard for all those years. *There is a better way!*

— James Dobson

December 22

Let love and faithfulness never leave you;
bind them around your neck,
write them on the tablet of your heart.
Proverbs 3:3

Passage for the Day: Proverbs 3:1–6

Genuine love is a gift we give others. It isn't purchased by their actions or contingent upon our emotions at the moment. It may carry with it strong emotional feelings, but it isn't supported by them. Rather, it is a decision we make on a daily basis that someone is special and valuable to us.

— Gary Smalley and
John Trent

January 27

But just as you excel in everything—in faith, in speech, in knowledge, in complete earnestness and in your love for us—see that you also excel in this grace of giving.
2 Corinthians 8:7

Passage for the Day: 2 Corinthians 8:1–9

As it happens, giving is to your benefit. It doesn't make you a saint or a martyr to give. In giving you are simply reflecting God's image—he who gave everything. Miserliness in all forms—monetary and emotional—diminishes us. The more we keep the less we have. And the less we are.

This is one of life's interesting paradoxes.

— **Daniel Taylor**

December 21

He replied, "If you have faith as small as a mustard seed, you can say to this mulberry tree, 'Be uprooted and planted in the sea,' and it will obey you."
Luke 17:6

Passage for the Day: Luke 17:1–10

We . . . can go through the valleys and mountains of our bereavement journey with "Father" on our lips. Our hearts may wonder, doubt and cry out in pain, but these feelings will not obliterate our faith. Even when we think we have lost that mustard seed, we do well to remember that our Father is faithful, for he has loved us first.

— **Philip W. Williams**

January 28

Then he said, "I am the God of your father,
the God of Abraham, the God of Isaac
and the God of Jacob." At this, Moses hid his face,
because he was afraid to look at God.
Exodus 3:6

Passage for the Day: Exodus 3:1–6

True Christian experience must always include a genuine encounter with God. Without this, religion is but a shadow, a reflection of reality, a cheap copy of the original once enjoyed by someone else of whom we have heard. . . . The spiritual giants of old were men who at some time became acutely conscious of the real Presence of God and maintained that consciousness for the rest of their lives.

— A.W. Tozer

December 20

A generous man will prosper;
he who refreshes others will himself be refreshed.
Proverbs 11:25

Passage for the Day: Proverbs 11:24–28

God has made us to be givers. It isn't something we *have* to do in order to please him so much as it's something we need to do to keep ourselves working properly. We are healthy and whole when we are both giving and receiving.

— **Daniel Taylor**

January 29

*Jesus looked at them and said,
"With man this is impossible, but with God
all things are possible."
Matthew 19:26*

Passage for the Day: Matthew 19:16–30

Does your problem seem bigger than life, bigger than God himself? It isn't. God is infinitely bigger than any problem you ever had or will have, and every time you call a problem unsolvable, you mock God. "With God all things are possible."

— Bill Hybels

December 19

He changes times and seasons;
he sets up kings and deposes them.
He gives wisdom to the wise and
knowledge to the discerning.
Daniel 2:21

Passage for the Day: Daniel 2:17–23

If . . . you cultivate vision—if, whenever you are faced with a problem, you immediately explore ways to deal with it—you will not only avert all sorts of discouragement, but you will also discover just how much creativity and wisdom God wants to give his children who look to him for help.

— Bill Hybels

January 30

The fear of the LORD is the beginning of wisdom;
all who follow his precepts have good understanding.
To him belongs eternal praise.
Psalm 111:10

Passage for the Day: Psalm 111:5–10

The conclusion of this psalm reminds me of Proverbs 1:7: "The fear (awesome respect) of the Lord is the beginning of knowledge." It seems that following his precepts in obedience should be the obvious outcome of my gratitude for all he's done for me!

— **Don Wyrtzen**

December 18

"If you love me, you will obey what I command."
John 14:15

Passage for the Day: John 14:15–31

The commandment of Jesus is not a sort of spiritual shock treatment. Jesus asks nothing of us without giving us the strength to perform it. His commandment never seeks to destroy life, but to foster, strengthen and heal it.

— **Dietrich Bonhoeffer**

January 31

*The weapons we fight with are not the weapons
of the world. On the contrary, they have
divine power to demolish strongholds.*
2 Corinthians 10:4

Passage for the Day: 2 Corinthians 10:1–6

With this authority a husband can pray against the dark forces he may feel pressing in on him and his family. He prays this way against sickness, against temptations, against forces in his community that would corrupt his children.

— Leonard LeSourd

December 17

I also shook out the folds of my robe and said, "In this way may God shake out of his house and possessions every man who does not keep this promise. So may such a man be shaken out and emptied!"

At this the whole assembly said, "Amen," and praised the LORD. And the people did as they had promised.
Nehemiah 5:13

Passage for the Day: Nehemiah 5:9–13

A Father has to be careful of his promises, because a real man will follow through. . . . The key is priorities. If you set a date with your child and something comes up at the office, you'd better see if you can postpone the office business. Otherwise, you're telling the child exactly where he fits in your life.

— **Mike Singletary**

February 1

*The LORD replied,
"My Presence will go with you, and
I will give you rest."
Exodus 33:14*

Passage for the Day: Exodus 33:12–23

A great many of the true saints of God have found their peak spiritual experiences in quietness and solitude. But many modern "saints" look for it only in exciting challenges or emotional catharsis. . . . [Many] confuse adrenalin arousal with spiritual growth. If their bodies were stimulated, they felt they were growing spiritually. If they were not stimulated, they felt nothing was happening.

— Archibald Hart

And he directed the people to sit down on the grass.
Taking the five loaves and the two fish and looking up
to heaven, he gave thanks and broke the loaves.
Then he gave them to the disciples, and
the disciples gave them to the people.
Matthew 14:19

Passage for the Day: Matthew 14:13–21

There are moments when we long for Christ to come again and feed the multitudes, not five thousand only, but fifty thousand, even fifty million. He could do it. Those first disciples had only two fish and a few loaves, but they gave him all they had. Is this not his word to us today—to give him all our loaves and fish, to give him everything we have? Then, who can say what he would be able to accomplish in our time
through us?

— Thomas Hale

February 2

He appointed twelve—designating them apostles—that
they might be with him and that he might
send them out to preach.
Mark 3:14

Passage for the Day: Mark 3:13–19

Notice that Jesus definitely called the apostles to *do*
something: to preach the gospel . . . . But his first call was for them
to *be someone*—his men. He wanted a mutually loving, nurturing,
caring relationship with these men.

— **Stephen Arterburn**
and David Stoop

December 15

But as for me, I watch in hope for the LORD,
I wait for God my Savior; my God will hear me.
Micah 7:7

Passage for the Day: Micah 7:5–7

God is looking for an opportunity to reveal himself to you,
so if you put him to the test and then watch for an answer without
too many preconceptions about how that answer will come, *I can
guarantee you* that you'll be in for some exciting surprises.

— Pat Boone

February 3

*Those who make them will be like them, and
so will all who trust in them.*
Psalm 115:8

Passage for the Day: Psalm 115:2–8

Idols are powerless. And work as an idol is just as powerless. Worst of all, those who worship work as an idol are defenseless in the face of true need. . . . I grieve with such men and women. They have chosen the wrong god. Of course, I also respect the fact that the same thing could happen to me as to anyone. It happens when we take God's gift of work and begin to worship and serve it rather than Christ.

— **Doug Sherman and
William Hendricks**

December 14

The man who says, "I know him,"
but does not do what he commands
is a liar, and the truth is not in him.
1 John 2:4

Passage for the Day: 1 John 2:3–6

There is a striking difference between knowing about God and knowing God. We may know the right God-words yet not experience God. Only in Jesus, the Son of God, can we truly know God the Father.

— **Reuben R. Welch**

February 4

Now I am ready to visit you for the third time, and I will not be a burden to you, because what I want is not your possessions but you. After all, children should not have to save up for their parents, but parents for their children.
2 Corinthians 12:14

Passage for the Day: 2 Corinthians 12:14–18

Once a parent, always a parent. Fathers and mothers alike, we don't stop caring just because we're no longer the main providers of shelter, food and the comforts of home. It's not merely our bounden duty, as *The Book of Common Prayer* says, as biological parents of these children; it's also our joyful pleasure to care for them, even after they no longer seem to need us.

— **D. Bruce Lockerbie**

December 13

Let the wicked forsake his way and the evil man his thoughts. Let him turn to the LORD, and he will have mercy on him, and to our God, for he will freely pardon.
Isaiah 55:7

Passage for the Day: Isaiah 55:1–7

Without the burden of past mistakes or anxiety about failing in the future, I'm free to concentrate on doing my very best in the present. And I believe that's how real, personal Christian faith can make it easier for anyone to reach his or her highest potential.
— **Tom Landry**

February 5

So he got up and ate and drank. Strengthened by that food, he traveled forty days and forty nights until he reached Horeb, the mountain of God.
1 Kings 19:8

Passage for the Day: 1 Kings 19:1–9

"You're not through yet, Elijah," [said the angel.]

"I'm going to send you from where you are to where I want you to be. I'm going to send you from the molehill to the mountain. . . . I'm going to send you from the wilderness to the mountain."

In the wilderness there is weakness, but on the mountain there is strength. In the wilderness there is loneliness, but on the mountain there is companionship. In the wilderness there is despair, but on the mountain there is hope.

— H. Beecher Hicks

December 12

The Lord is gracious and compassionate,
slow to anger and rich in love.
Psalm 145:8

Passage for the Day: Psalm 145:8–16

God's ways are not our ways. We are so selfish. He is so self-giving, so self-sharing! We are so short-tempered. He is so patient, so persevering! We are so hard and critical. He is so merciful and kind.

— **W. Phillip Keller**

February 6

*"In the same way, on the outside
you appear to people as righteous but on the inside
you are full of hypocrisy and wickedness."
Matthew 23:28*

Passage for the Day: Matthew 23:25–28

You and I as Christians need to realize that however acceptable our lives may be for the general audience, we still possess an R-rated heart, and we're as good as dead if we want God to meet us on any other ground than his grace and forgiveness.

The joy of this truth is that once I can believe that forgiveness for myself, then I can believe it for anybody. I have new eyes to see beyond my neighbor's sin and love him or her with the love of Christ.

— John Fischer

December 11

*"But I tell you that anyone who looks at
a woman lustfully has already committed
adultery with her in his heart."*
Matthew 5:28

Passage for the Day: Matthew 5:27–30

A one-woman kind of man has purposefully cultivated a
special kind of blindness.

— Steve Farrar

February 7

I delight in your decrees;
I will not neglect your word.
Psalm 119:16

Passage for the Day: Psalm 119:9–16

The gospel of Jesus Christ must be the bad news of the conviction of sin before it can be the Good News of redemption. The truth is revealed in God's Holy Word; life can be lived only in absolute and disciplined submission to its authority.

— Charles Colson

December 10

May your unfailing love be my comfort,
according to your promise to your servant.
Psalm 119:76

Passage for the Day: Psalm 119:73–80

When life caves in, you do not need reasons, you need comfort. You do not need some answers, you need some*one*.

And Jesus does not come to us with an explanation; he comes to us with his presence.

— Bob Benson

February 8

*Who gave himself for our sins to rescue us from
the present evil age, according to the will
of our God and Father.*
Galatians 1:4

Passage for the Day: Galatians 1:1–5

This caliber of divine love eludes us mortals. We are, for the most part, so selfish, so self-centered, so self-preoccupied, we recoil from those spike-torn hands extended to us in mercy, compassion and deep longing. We simply refuse to believe anyone truly can care for us with such pure motives.

— **W. Phillip Keller**

December 9

So we rebuilt the wall till all of it reached half its height, for the people worked with all their heart.
Nehemiah 4:6

Passage for the Day: Nehemiah 4:6–20

Work done for personal gain dulls my spirit; work that produces something beyond myself excites me.

Inviting God into my work opens the door for new creativity.

Being in the right job, doing the kind of work where I give more than I receive brings a whole new light onto my strength as a man.

— Leonard LeSourd

February 9

*When Moses came down from Mount Sinai with the
two tablets of the Testimony in his hands,
he was not aware that his face was radiant
because he had spoken with the LORD.*
Exodus 34:29

Passage for the Day: Exodus 34:29–35

I think of something [my wife] Popie says about God: how
you can worry that your relationship with him has gone cold, that
you've lost your spiritual edge. You can think it will take a lot of
time, a month or so of spiritual discipline, to get going again with
him.

Then you sit down and discover, in just minutes, that you
don't have to do a thing—except take some time. Be alone with him.
In what feels like no time you are caught up again in your love.

— **Tim Stafford**

December 8

Religion that God our Father accepts as pure and faultless is this: to look after orphans and widows in their distress and to keep oneself from being polluted by the world.
James 1:27

Passage for the Day: James 1:22–27

The clear duty of real men goes beyond "live and let live." We are mandated to protect widows, orphans, the alien and all those who lack sustaining relationships. As long as men and boys fail to be protective, they will fall prey to the typical male sexual fantasy that sells [pornographic] magazines and films. . . .

The only real solution is to teach boys that the source of their power is in the nurturing and protecting image of God created within them. When we express our essential nature, then substitutes, like pornographic fantasies, lose their appeal.

— E. James Wilder

February 10

As he walked along, he saw Levi son of Alphaeus sitting at the tax collector's booth. "Follow me," Jesus told him, and Levi got up and followed him.
Mark 2:14

Passage for the Day: Mark 2:13–17

Jesus summons men to follow him, not as a teacher or pattern of the good life, but as the Christ, the Son of God. In this short text Jesus Christ and his claim are proclaimed to men. Not a word of praise is given to the disciple for his decision for Christ. We are not expected to contemplate the disciple, but only him who calls, and his absolute authority.

— Dietrich Bonhoeffer

December 7

He restores my soul. He guides me in paths of
righteousness for his name's sake.
Psalm 23:3

Passage for the Day: Psalm 23:1–6

A well-loved king of Israel wrote, "Even though I walk through the valley of the shadow of death, . . . you are with me" [Psalm 23:4]. In that relationship with God, experienced by thousands of men and women like ourselves, can be found a hub [an eternal center] that no experience in life can destroy.

— **Haddon W. Robinson**

February 11

And pleaded earnestly with him,
"My little daughter is dying. Please come
and put your hands on her so that
she will be healed and live."
Mark 5:23

Passage for the Day: Mark 5:21–24, 35–43

That daughter of yours wants to see in you an intelligent man's viewpoint about life, plus the ability to head up the family in fatherly ways. Then she can really love you as her father as well as a fine man. . . . You are the most important man in her young life.

— **John E. Crawford**

December 6

Who is wise and understanding among you?
Let him show it by his good life, by deeds done in the
humility that comes from wisdom.
James 3:13

Passage for the Day: James 3:13–18

O Divine Master, grant that I may not
so much seek to be consoled as to console;
to be understood as to understand;
to be loved as to love;
for it is in giving that we receive;
it is in pardoning that we are pardoned;
and it is in dying that we are born to Eternal Life.

— Francis of Assisi

February 12

And over all these virtues put on love,
which binds them all together in perfect unity.
Colossians 3:14

Passage for the Day: Colossians 3:12–14

Love that is at liberty to be realistic calls us to recognize that marriage is something that must be worked out. . . . As one elderly lady testified, "Love is what you go through together." It is the recognition, therefore, that you have some needs which are not going to be met by the other person, and that there are some things upon which you will never totally agree. Realism demands patience and a willingness to adjust. The art of marriage, it has been said, is in maintaining equilibrium through the various changes and adjustments of life together.

— G.R. Slater

December 5

*"Can a mother forget the baby at her breast and have no
compassion on the child she has borne? Though
she may forget, I will not forget you!"*
Isaiah 49:15

Passage for the Day: Isaiah 49:13–18

To believe means to realize not just with the head but also
with the heart that God loves *me* in a creative, intimate, unique,
reliable and *tender* way.

— **Brennan Manning**

February 13

He is to lay both hands on the head of the live goat and confess over it all the wickedness and rebellion of the Israelites—all their sins—and put them on the goat's head. He shall send the goat away into the desert in the care of a man appointed for the task.
Leviticus 16:21

Passage for the Day: Leviticus 16:20–22

God placed on Jesus the sin of the world: our rejection of God. . . . He absorbed our full rejection, sacrificing his life to it. When the anger was absorbed, it lost its power. Then we could begin anew, forgiven by him.

— **Tim Stafford**

December 4

"So, because you are luke-warm—neither hot nor cold—I am about to spit you out of my mouth."
Revelation 3:16

Passage for the Day: Revelation 3:14–22

As long as Jesus is one of many options, he is no option. . . . And as long as you can take him or leave him, you might as well leave him, because he won't be taken half-heartedly.

— Max Lucado

February 14

"Not so with you. Instead, whoever wants to become great among you must be your servant."
Matthew 20:26

Passage for the Day: Matthew 20:20–28

A real man will treat his wife right. He will be a servant rather than a master. He will do the right thing because it's the right thing. He will give a hundred percent no matter what he's called upon to do.

And how will a man know when he's a real man? When he seeks to serve. When he can sit down with his wife and honestly look to fulfill her needs before his own. He should ask, "What can I do for you?"

— **Mike Singletary**

December 3

One thing I ask of the LORD, this is what I seek:
that I may dwell in the house of the LORD all the days of
my life, to gaze upon the beauty of the LORD and to
seek him in his temple.
Psalm 27:4

Passage for the Day: Psalm 27:1–6

Help me to understand that only a few things really *are*
necessary in life. And when you get right down to it, only one: to sit
at your feet . . . listening . . . looking into your eyes . . . and loving
you.

— **Ken Gire**

February 15

*Unless the LORD builds the house,
its builders labor in vain. Unless the LORD
watches over the city, the watchmen
stand guard in vain.
Psalm 127:1*

Passage for the Day: Psalm 127:1–5

Many feel that by working longer hours they can provide more things to bring happiness to their home or afford a nicer, newer home in hopes that it will bring happiness. . . . It doesn't satisfy that empty longing in the pit of our soul, that longing for a home, a *real* home—a home where love thrives, lush and fragrant. The reason why it's futile burning the candle at both ends—rising early, staying up late—is that God, not our labors, is the source of our blessing.

— **Charles Swindoll**

December 2

*"Just as the Son of Man did not come to be served,
but to serve, and to give his life as a ransom for many."*
Matthew 20:28

Passage for the Day: Matthew 20:20–28

The long painful history of the church is the history of
people ever and again tempted to choose power over love, control
over the cross, being a leader over being led. Those who resisted this
temptation to the end and thereby give us hope are the true saints.

— Henri Nouwen

February 16

*For it is by grace you have been saved, through faith—
and this not from yourselves, it is the gift of God.
Ephesians 2:8*

Passage for the Day: Ephesians 2:1–10

[The Muslim passenger in our car] told me how, as a student of Western civilization, he had read about the Reformation . . . on the issue of justification by faith in Jesus Christ—not by the Church's system of works.

"When I read it," he said, "I knew that this was the true way. Doing good works is one of the main tenets of Islam; without good works a person could never get to heaven. But anyone who has really tried to be good knows himself well enough to know he could never be good enough. So I became a believer in Jesus Christ."

— Mark Ritchie

December 1

"You asked, 'Who is this that obscures my counsel without knowledge?' Surely I spoke of things I did not understand, things too wonderful for me to know."
Job 42:3

Passage for the Day: Job 42:1–6

We are always seeking the reason. We want to know why. Like Job, we finally want God to tell us just what is going on. . . .

But God does not reveal his plan, he reveals himself. He comes to us as warmth when we are cold, fellowship when we are alone, strength when we are weak, peace when we are troubled, courage when we are afraid, songs when we are sad, and bread when we are hungry.

— Bob Benson

February 17

" 'Do not seek revenge or bear a grudge
against one of your people,
but love your neighbor as yourself.
I am the LORD.' "
Leviticus 19:18

Passage for the Day: Leviticus 19:9–18

When Jesus was asked to name the great commandments in the Scriptures, he didn't hesitate in the least. He told a young lawyer, "Love the Lord your God with all your heart and with all your soul and with all your mind . . . Love your neighbor as yourself" (Matthew 22:37,39). Loving God, loving others and finding value in ourselves. Without a doubt, these three aspects of love are the most effective weapons against the destructive power of low self-worth.

— **Gary Smalley and
John Trent**

November 30

*So in Christ we who are many form one body, and
each member belongs to all the others.*
Romans 12:5

Passage for the Day: Romans 12:3–8

In spite of the pain, frustration and embarrassment, the unavoidable world of life in the family is still God's gift. The caring, nurture and confidence that comes from being seen at our worst and still knowing that we belong is his gift to us. It is the place where we can . . . love one another over the long haul. It is a place where we see his power and grace demonstrated over and over again.

— **John F. Westfall**

February 18

*After six days Jesus took Peter, James and John with
him and led them up a high mountain, where they were
all alone. There he was transfigured before them.*
Mark 9:2

Passage for the Day: Mark 9:2–13

You don't need to be a friend to everyone. Remember the
model of Jesus. He preached to, ministered to, and healed thousands
of people, but he only had twelve disciples. Of those twelve, only
three were invited with him when he was transfigured on the
mountain. . . .

It's one thing to reach out to a needy person, but it's
another to have a friendship. In the first situation you're doing
social work or a spiritual ministry of caring. When you are truly a
friend, you and your friend will be giving equally to each other.

— **Jim Conway**

*I want to know Christ and the power of his resurrection
and the fellowship of sharing in his sufferings,
becoming like him in his death.*
Philippians 3:10

Passage for the Day: Philippians 3:7–11

I want more than anything in the world for Jesus Christ to live out his life through me. Without him I am nothing; with him I have the promise of everlasting life. . . . Does anything else give you that assurance? It boggles my mind that someone can see life breathed into a baby, watch the grass die and then come to life again, see leaves fall and watch the rebirth of a tree, or gaze on any of the majestic splendor that is this earth and not be overpowered by the presence of an Almighty God!

— Bill McCartney

February 19

*To all perfection I see a limit; but
your commands are boundless.
Psalm 119:96*

Passage for the Day: Psalm 119:89–96

To live life to its fullest and truly enjoy it, we need to understand and abide by the rules God spells out in the Bible. God isn't out to spoil our fun; he knows that life without limits results in anarchy and misery. It's only when we have absolute limits that we can be truly free to enjoy the best life has to offer.

— Tom Landry

November 28

*For you died, and your life is now hidden
with Christ in God.
Colossians 3:3*

Passage for the Day: Colossians 3:1–4

Only when we die to self can we fully love one another.
— Judson Edwards

February 20

From him the whole body, joined and held together
by every supporting ligament, grows and
builds itself up in love, as each part does its work.
Ephesians 4:16

Passage for the Day: Ephesians 4:1–16

The Body of Christ, like our own bodies, is composed of individual, unlike cells that are knit together to form one Body. He is the whole thing, and the joy of the Body increases as individual cells realize they can be diverse without becoming isolated outposts.

— **Paul Brand**

November 27

"You are my friends if you do what I command."
John 15:14

Passage for the Day: John 15:9–17

Jesus does not present himself to us as "holier than thou," but rather as a friend. He said, "I no longer call you servants, because a servant does not know his master's business. Instead, I have called you friends, for everything that I learned from my Father I have made known to you" (John 15:15).

— **Jim Conway**

February 21

"The LORD turn his face toward you
and give you peace."
Numbers 6:26

Passage for the Day: Numbers 6:22–27

I was shocked at how radically they had cut the arm back. The incision started at my neck and went in a diagonal to my underarm area. The arm was gone. The shoulder was gone. The shoulder blade was gone. And the left side of my collar bone was gone.

"Okay, God. This is what I've got to live with. Put this behind me; let me go forward."

And when the one-armed man looked back at me [in the mirror], there was peace in his eyes.

— **Dave Dravecky**

November 26

*But Stephen, full of the Holy Spirit,
looked up to heaven and saw the glory of God,
and Jesus standing at the right hand of God.
Acts 7:55*

Passage for the Day: Acts 7:54—8:1

I'm part of the fellowship of the unashamed. I have the Holy Spirit power. The die has been cast. I have stepped over the line. The decision has been made—I'm a disciple of his. I won't look back, let up, slow down, back away, or be still. My past is redeemed, my present makes sense, my future is secure. I'm finished and done now with low living, sight walking, smooth knees, colorless dreams, tamed visions, worldly talking, cheap giving and dwarfed goals.

> — **A young pastor in
> Zimbabwe, Africa,
> later martyred for
> his faith in Christ.**

*"Therefore what God had joined together,
let man not separate."*
Mark 10:9

Passage for the Day: Mark 10:1–12

Jesus announces the warning in the face of easy divorce in his teaching . . . He restates the Genesis 2 picture of one man and one woman forming one flesh unity, and suggests that the only alternative to the kind of beautiful sexual intimacy is holy celibacy: being single for the glory of God and the service of God's purposes in the world.

— **Donald M. Joy**

November 25

*"Take my yoke upon you and learn from me, for
I am gentle and humble in heart, and
you will find rest for your souls."*
Matthew 11:29

Passage for the Day: Matthew 11:25–30

The subtle shift from trust in Christ to our own self-efforts
robs us of hope and joy. We begin to tally hurts, count
disappointments and weigh sacrifices. And already the drift has set
in. We need the warning, but more than that, we need to know that
we are known, understood and loved by someone who has marked
out the path, has won the victory and is with us on the way. That
someone is Jesus.

— **Reuben R. Welch**

February 23

Out of the depths I cry to you, O LORD.
Psalm 130:1

Passage for the Day: Psalm 130:1–8

The Biblical Christian can only pray empty-handed, as the thirteenth-century Dominican preacher William Peraldus expressed it. Or, as Augustine observed, "The best disposition for praying is that of being desolate, forsaken, stripped of everything."

— Donald Bloesch

November 24

*Let the peace of Christ rule in your hearts,
since as members of one body you were called
to peace. And be thankful.*
Colossians 3:15

Passage for the Day: Colossians 3:15–17

The magic of a thankful spirit is that it has the power to
replace anger with love, resentment with happiness, fear with faith,
worry with peace, the desire to dominate with the wish to play on a
team, self-preoccupation with concern for the needs of others, guilt
with an open door to forgiveness, sexual impurity with honor and
respect, jealousy with joy at another's success, lack of creativity with
inspired productivity, inferiorities with dignity, a lack of love with
an abundance of self-sharing.

— **Donald E. Demaray**

February 24

For to me, to live is Christ and to die is gain.
Philippians 1:21

Passage for the Day: Philippians 1:18–26

We die because we have lived. We live in order to know and love the God who made us. In dying we become more real than we ever can while part of this sorrowful world. I will die someday, and so will you. And that is a good thing.

— Daniel Taylor

November 23

*"This is to be a lasting ordinance for you: Atonement is
to be made once a year for all the sins of the Israelites."
And it was done, as the LORD commanded Moses.*
Leviticus 16:34

Passage for the Day: Leviticus 16:29–34

The big picture is simply this. People turned their backs on
God and God immediately went to work to regain fellowship.
Observations from the Old Testament should be enough to convince
us that God is a God of love and forgiveness.

— **Charles Stanley**

February 25

Not one of you will enter the land I swore with uplifted hand to make your home, except Caleb son of Jephunneh and Joshua son of Nun.
Numbers 14:30

Passage for the Day: Numbers 13:26–14:9

God doesn't like it—not at all [that ten of the spies into Canaan were frightened of the Canaanites]. . . . He tells Moses the bad news. Not *one* of those who complained, not one of those who are over twenty years old, will ever make it to the promised land.

That's their punishment for faithlessness. A whole new generation of Israelites will have to be born into the kind of strong faith that their parents lack. Then, God's chosen people will make it.

What the Israelites forgot—and what we easily forget—is that faith can move mountains.

— **James Schaap**

November 22

All you have made will praise you, O LORD;
your saints will extol you.
Psalm 145:10

Passage for the Day: Psalm 145:8–16

Father . . . we are thankful for the reminders you give us daily in the form of our children. Reminders, first, of your generosity, for children are a gift from you. But reminders, as well, of our finitude, or our place in this world that you have created. Reminders that we are stewards of your creation, not its gods. Reminders that we tend the seeds that you have sown, but we do not determine the plant's growth. Reminders that our final duty is to honor you through our acts of service to one another, not to serve and honor ourselves.

— S.D. Gaede

"To love him with all your heart, with all your understanding and with all your strength, and to love your neighbor as yourself is more important than all burnt offerings and sacrifices."
Mark 12:33

Passage for the Day: Mark 12:28–34

The only way we know to help our Nepali friends in a lasting way is to put them in touch with the God who is the source of love and who sent his Son Jesus into the world to demonstrate it.

We know from personal experience that God's love changes lives; the faith we share with our Nepali friends is not a hand-me-down or merely theoretical faith. His love changed our lives and sent us to Nepal; his love has kept us here.

— Thomas Hale

November 21

Be devoted to one another in brotherly love.
Honor one another above yourselves.
Romans 12:10

Passage for the Day: Romans 12:9–13

Like genuine love, honor is a gift we give to someone. It involves the decision we make *before* we put love into action that a person is of high value. In fact, love for someone often begins to flow once we have made the decision to honor him.

— **Gary Smalley and**
John Trent

February 27

O LORD, you have searched me
and you know me.
Psalm 139:1

Passage for the Day: Psalm 139:1–24

I am not an enigma to [God]. I am one whom he has known since conception. Consequently, he does not reject or despise me. Rather, he begins now to re-create me in his own lovely likeness.
— **W. Phillip Keller**

November 20

That is why I am suffering as I am. Yet I am not ashamed, because I know whom I have believed, and am convinced that he is able to guard what I have entrusted to him for that day.
2 Timothy 1:12

Passage for the Day: 2 Timothy 1:3–12

Failures teach us that to wait on God is not only to wait *for* his mercy, but to wait *by* his mercy. . . . The glory hidden in our failures is the discovery that the very thing we wait for is what we wait by! The success of our waiting lies not in who we are, but in who God is. It is not our strength that will pull us through to the end, it is God's amazing grace and mercy.

— Ben Patterson

February 28

*Do nothing out of selfish ambition
or vain conceit, but in humility
consider others better than yourselves.
Philippians 2:3*

Passage for the Day: Philippians 2:1–11

That one verse contains more wisdom than most marriage manuals combined. If heeded, it could virtually eliminate divorce from the catalog of human experience.

— James Dobson

November 19

*Above all, love each other deeply, because
love covers over a multitude of sins.
1 Peter 4:8*

Passage for the Day: 1 Peter 4:7–11

I pray . . . for the ability to translate

    the message of God's eternal love into
        words
that will pierce the benumbed minds of
        busy men
and move their hearts to faith and
        obedience.

— Leslie Brandt

February 29

"You shall not commit adultery."
Deuteronomy 5:18

Passage for the Day: Deuteronomy 5:16–21

If you are in miserable [marital] circumstances as you read these words, you obviously feel as though you are stuck with small potatoes. But if you will honor God by being obedient, he will honor you by throwing you some kind of banquet. I can't tell you how, I can't tell you when, but I can tell you that he keeps his word. He is the God of surprises, and if you remain faithful in that tough marriage, he will surprise you one day with joy.

— **Steve Farrar**

November 18

I love you, O L<small>ORD</small>, my strength.
Psalm 18:1

Passage for the Day: Psalm 18:1–6

We can be certain that it is quite impossible to worship God without loving him. Scripture and reason agree to declare this. And God is never satisfied with anything less than all.

— A.W. Tozer

March 1

"And he will go on before the Lord, in the spirit and power of Elijah, to turn the hearts of the fathers to their children and the disobedient to the wisdom of the righteous—to make ready a people prepared for the Lord."
Luke 1:17

Passage for the Day: Luke 1:8–17

Every girl needs a father she can talk to, argue with, race at a picnic, play ball with in the cool of the evening, hug and kiss. These things are worth doing even if you have to make room in your time schedule. She is growing up just as swiftly as you are adding years to yourself. Waiting until next year or the year after that will find her older and that much less inclined to talk or swim or go to the concert with you.

— **John E. Crawford**

November 17

"Ask and it will be given to you;
seek and you will find;
knock and the door will be opened to you."
Matthew 7:7

Passage for the Day: Matthew 7:7–12

Just as surely as we are looking in different ways, answers are coming to us in a diversity which reflects the mystery of God himself. The wonderful thing is that he is making certain we are receiving and that we are finding and that doors are being opened to us.

— **Bob Benson**

March 2

Let the morning bring me word of your unfailing love,
for I have put my trust in you. Show me
the way I should go, for to you I lift up my soul.
Psalm 143:8

Passage for the Day: Psalm 143:1–12

O Lord, fill me with your Spirit today. Guide me, enable me, teach me, comfort me. I need help as I continue my pilgrimage.
— Don Wyrtzen

November 16

For it is written:
"Be holy, because I am holy."
1 Peter 1:16

Passage for the Day: 1 Peter 1:13–16

       The saint . . . seeks not his own glory but the glory of God. And in order that God may be glorified in all things, the saint wishes himself to be nothing but a pure instrument of the divine will. He wants himself to be simply a window through which God's mercy shines on the world. And for this he strives to be holy.

— **Thomas Merton**

March 3

Be on your guard; stand firm in the faith;
be men of courage; be strong.
1 Corinthians 16:13

Passage for the Day: 1 Corinthians 16:13–14

It . . . takes relational courage to build significant
relationships with friends, to look another person in the eye and say,
"Isn't it time we stopped talking about the weather and the stock
market and started talking about what's going on in your life and
mine? Isn't it time we became brothers?" Not many men have the
courage to challenge each other, to fight for each other's spiritual
and relational growth.

— **Bill Hybels**

November 15

*We were therefore buried with him through baptism
into death in order that, just as Christ
was raised from the dead through the glory
of the Father, we too may live a new life.*
Romans 6:4

Passage for the Day: Romans 5:20–6:14

All of us who have been baptized in Christ and have "put on
Christ" as a new identity are bound to be holy as he is holy. We are
bound to live worthy lives, and our actions should bear witness to
our union with him. He should manifest his presence in us and
through us.

— **Thomas Merton**

March 4

*I press on toward the goal to win the prize for which
God has called me heavenward in Christ Jesus.
Philippians 3:14*

Passage for the Day: Philippians 3:12–16

It is our relationship with God in life that enables us to make sense out of seeming nonsense. Even when sense and purpose seem to escape us, we trust that one day we will understand. On that day we will come face to face with the author of life.

— Philip W. Williams

November 14

People who want to get rich fall into temptation and a
trap and into many foolish and harmful desires that
plunge men into ruin and destruction.
1 Timothy 6:9

Passage for the Day: 1 Timothy 6:3–10

Men who opt to be satisfied with what they possess will
have more time and energy for the kinds of nurturing relationships
that will meet their basic needs.

— Stephen Arterburn
and David Stoop

March 5

And now, O Israel, what does the L<small>ORD</small> your God ask of you but to fear the L<small>ORD</small> your God, to walk in all his ways, to love him, to serve the L<small>ORD</small> your God with all your heart and with all your soul.
Deuteronomy 10:12

Passage for the Day: Deuteronomy 10:12–13

Everything about you is to be involved in loving God. It makes sense that your work must be involved as well. Just think about how much of your heart, soul and might go into your work. Imagine, then, as you spend yourself at that task, being able to say, "I'm here to do something God wants done, and I intend to do it because I love him." The person who can make this statement has turned his work into one of his primary means of obeying the greatest of God's commandments.

— **Doug Sherman and William Hendricks**

November 13

Where is the wise man? Where is the scholar?
Where is the philosopher of this age?
Has not God made foolish the wisdom of the world?
1 Corinthians 1:20

Passage for the Day: 1 Corinthians 1:20–31

Everyone who comes to know Jesus stumbles because of him. He fails to meet our wrong expectations. He calls us to do impossible things or to become something we think we could never become. This is his way of teaching us how much we need him. He breaks us to pieces so that he can put us back together in his image.

— **Michael Card**

March 6

"Give, and it will be given to you. A good measure,
pressed down, shaken together and running over,
will be poured into your lap. For with the measure
you use, it will be measured to you."
Luke 6:38

Passage for the Day: Luke 6:37–42

The richest people I know are those who have given
themselves unselfishly to other people. Such motivation will affect
the way you sell, cook, teach or ply your particular trade. True
riches, of course, are totally unrelated to money or material reward.
In fact, if a person has earned money without helping people, his
money will not buy him happiness.

— **Tim LaHaye**

November 12

Blessed is the man who makes the LORD his trust,
who does not look to the proud, to those
who turn aside to false gods.
Psalm 40:4

Passage for the Day: Psalm 40:4–10

Each of us can change our own little world. Fathers who are honest with themselves will admit that we all make mistakes. We have all made bad decisions. Some of those decisions have to be reversed. If you have accepted a promotion and a transfer that takes you a step up the corporate ladder at the expense of your kids, maybe you need to think about taking a step back. More important than providing a life of ease for your kids is making sure they know you love them unconditionally.

— **Mike Singletary**

March 7

The fear of the LORD is the beginning of knowledge,
but fools despise wisdom and discipline.
Proverbs 1:7

Passage for the Day: Proverbs 1:1–7

The true test of knowledge, according to Proverbs, goes
beyond academic achievement to moral responsibility. It zeroes in
on decision-making and shows itself best in the disciplining of the
character; this results in "a disciplined and prudent life." To live
prudently means to think clearly about one's choices and arrive at
decisions controlled not by whim or appetite but by an
understanding of the difference between right and wrong. This is
what Proverbs also calls "discretion" or "discernment."

— **D. Bruce Lockerbie**

November 11

*But do not forget this one thing, dear friends: With the
Lord a day is like a thousand years, and
a thousand years are like a day.*
2 Peter 3:8

Passage for the Day: 2 Peter 3:8–16

Redemption in Jesus Christ initiates a new life, one in
which the life of God invades ours, making the passage of time take
on the significance of eternity.

— **William T.
McConnell**

March 8

Do not be anxious about anything, but in everything, by prayer and petition, with thanksgiving, present your requests to God.
Philippians 4:6

Passage for the Day: Philippians 4:2–9

[Paul] does not deny that the worst things will happen finally to all of us, as indeed he must have had a strong suspicion they were soon to happen to him. He does not try to minimize them. He does not try to explain them away as God's will or God's judgment or God's method of testing our spiritual fiber. He simply tells the Philippians that in spite of them—even in the thick of them—they are to keep in constant touch with the One who unimaginably transcends the worst things as he also unimaginably transcends the best.

— Frederick
Buechner

November 10

*For we know that our old self was crucified with him so
that the body of sin might be done away with,
that we should no longer be slaves to sin.
Romans 6:6*

Passage for the Day: Romans 6:5–7

I am personally convinced that this submission, this dying
to self, this crucifying of pride [see Philippians 2:1–8] is crucial to
our joy. We think of denying self as somber, grim-faced business
when it is in truth a prelude to dancing. If you want power, learn to
be assertive. If you want joy, learn to be submissive.

— Judson Edwards

March 9

However, there should be no poor among you,
for in the land the LORD your God is giving you to possess
as your inheritance, he will richly bless you.
Deuteronomy 15:4

Passage for the Day: Deuteronomy 15:1–11

The contest for America's moral leadership is still going on; whether the church is willing and able to step up to its Biblical responsibility is still to be decided. It may be the greatest question we face. For if we fail even the simple test of responding to human needs in our own community, what possible claim will we have to assume a role of genuine moral leadership in society? We dare not fail.

— **Charles Colson**

For your Maker is your husband—the L ORD Almighty is his name—the Holy One of Israel is your Redeemer; he is called the God of all the earth.
Isaiah 54:5

Passage for the Day: Isaiah 54:4–8

Every marriage needs the miracle of God's presence. It needs to invite him in so that he can introduce his reconciling grace into the material of two lives. That grace is not a buttress thrown up from the outside to hold up the walls of marriage when they are unable to stand by themselves. It is the "glue" which provides the conditions of personal responsibility, patience and understanding by which two persons adhere to each other in willing faithfulness.

— **G.R. Slater**

March 10

*After this, Jesus went out and saw a tax collector
by the name of Levi sitting at his tax booth.
"Follow me," Jesus said to him, and Levi got up,
left everything and followed him.*
Luke 5:27

Passage for the Day: Luke 5:27–32

To each of his disciples, Jesus simply said, "Follow me."
That was an invitation, not a requirement. An invitation respects
the freedom of the invitee to accept or decline. Indeed, the "no"
answer is perhaps the greatest expression of human dignity
possible. That men and women can go to heaven is an expression of
God's love; that they can go to hell is an expression of the value he
places on their freedom.

— **John Fischer**

November 8

We are glad whenever we are weak but you are strong;
and our prayer is for your perfection.
2 Corinthians 13:9

Passage for the Day: 2 Corinthians 13:1–10

Come on guys! Let us at least try to struggle honestly. We need to be confronted by our actions, messages and shortcomings if we expect to learn and grow. No more hiding behind excuses. No blaming others. No hiding behind phrases like, "This is just the way I am." Let us have a look at who we are for that is the best indication of who our sons will become.

— E. James Wilder

March 11

*For the Lord gives wisdom, and from his mouth
come knowledge and understanding.*
Proverbs 2:6

Passage for the Day: Proverbs 2:1–11

It is my God-appointed task to ensure that my sons will be ready to lead a family. I must equip them to that end. Little boys are the hope of the next generation. They are the fathers of tomorrow. They must know who they are and what they are to do. They must see their role model in action. That's how they will know what it means to be a male. That puts the ball in my court . . . and in yours.

— **Steve Farrar**

"Son of man, say to the ruler of Tyre, 'This is what the Sovereign LORD says: "'In the pride of your heart you say, "I am a god; I sit on the throne of a god in the heart of the seas." But you are a man and not a god, though you think you are as wise as a god.'"'"
Ezekiel 28:2

Passage for the Day: Ezekiel 28:1–10

Desiring our own good is not sinful in itself, but natural and instinctive. God gave us everything, even our very existence. He wants us to take care of what he gave us. It is the act of putting ourselves at the center of the universe, where God belongs, that is unqualified sin. This is, in fact, the very definition of sin.

— Larry Crabb

So then, just as you received
Christ Jesus as Lord, continue to live in him.
Colossians 2:6

Passage for the Day: Colossians 2:6–12

Jesus is the answer, and it's precisely *because* he is the answer that we can venture out. Because he is Lord of all, we can walk into all and find him Lord. This is not only a privilege, it's a mandate. It's what Christians are called to do in the world.

— John Fischer

November 6

He is the image of the invisible God, the firstborn over all creation.
Colossians 1:15

Passage for the Day: Colossians 1:15–20

In our rating-conscious society that ranks everything from baseball teams to "the best chili in New York," an attitude of relative worth can easily seep into the church of Christ. But the design of the group of people who follow Jesus should not resemble a military machine or a corporate structure. The church Jesus founded is much more like a family in which the son retarded from birth has as much worth as his brother the Rhodes scholar. It is like the body composed of cells most striking in their diversity but most effective in their mutuality.

— **Paul Brand**

March 13

Remember how the LORD your God led you all the way in the desert these forty years, to humble you and to test you in order to know what was in your heart, whether or not you would keep his commands.
Deuteronomy 8:2

Passage for the Day: Deuteronomy 8:1–5

[Having been confronted by pain] I remind myself that all these toys were never intended to possess my heart, that my true good is in another world and my only real treasure is Christ. And perhaps, by God's grace, I succeed, and for a day or two become a creature consciously dependent on God and drawing its strength from the right sources. But the moment the threat is withdrawn, my whole nature leaps back to the toys. . . . The terrible necessity of tribulation is only too clear. God has had me for but forty-eight hours and then only by dint of taking everything else away from me.

— **C.S. Lewis**

November 5

A friend loves at all times, and a
brother is born for adversity.
Proverbs 17:17

Passage for the Day: Proverbs 17:17–22

In your life you should always have some people whom you
nourish and who return little or nothing to you. You should also
have people who nourish you, but you may return nothing to them.
A third kind of relationship is equal sharing. This is friendship.

— **Jim Conway**

March 14

"I tell you, among those born of women there is no one greater than John; yet the one who is least in the kingdom of God is greater than he."
Luke 7:28

Passage for the Day: Luke 7:24–28

[One] characteristic which qualified John as a real man was his vision. In describing him, Jesus had asked, "What did you go out into the desert to see? . . . A prophet? Yes, I tell you, and more than a prophet" [Luke 7:24,26].

What is a prophet? . . . He has been given the perspective of God himself and is able to see the meaning behind events. Unfortunately . . . all we are interested in is an immediate solution to a present problem. So we need to develop the ability to see the consequences of our actions—to see past the immediate to the ultimate.

— D. Stuart Briscoe

November 4

What, after all, is Apollos? And what is Paul? Only servants, through whom you came to believe—as the Lord has assigned to each his task.
1 Corinthians 3:5

Passage for the Day: 1 Corinthians 3:5–15

We must dispense with the myth that commitment to Christ means becoming a clergyman, or that work done inside a church building or in a church organization is more holy, somehow, than work done in the marketplace. Christ came to give us a sense of calling in everyday work. This is where the world is changed, and where the kingdom is built.

— **Bruce Larson**

March 15

*In all your ways acknowledge him, and
he will make your paths straight.
Proverbs 3:6*

Passage for the Day: Proverbs 3:1–6

Cowards do not last long on their spiritual pilgrimages. They shrivel up and disappear. It takes enormous courage to repent and become a Christian. It takes enormous courage to follow God's leadings in the Christian life. Some of his callings demand the best you can summon. Some of his tests stretch you to the limit. Some of his adventures evoke great fears and doubts. Truly, spiritual courage is on the endangered character-quality list.

— **Bill Hybels**

November 3

Finally, brothers, whatever is true, whatever is noble, whatever is right, whatever is pure, whatever is lovely, whatever is admirable—if anything is excellent or praiseworthy—think about such things.
Philippians 4:8

Passage for the Day: Philippians 4:4–9

Prayer is one of the unlimited resources available to each of us. In this bound-up world, prayer may be a lost art, but it is always the starting point when we move toward God. In prayer we set aside our agendas, letting God's priorities become our priorities, and we receive his resources.

— **John F. Westfall**

March 16

*Put to death, therefore, whatever belongs
to your earthly nature: sexual immorality, impurity,
lust, evil desires and greed, which is idolatry.*
Colossians 3:5

Passage for the Day: Colossians 3:5–11

No one is immune. You're not. I'm not. Lust is no respecter of persons. . . . It's alluring voice can infiltrate the most intelligent mind and cause its victim to believe its lies and respond to its appeal. And beware—it never gives up. . . . If you get yourself into a situation that leaves you defenseless and weak, if your door is left even slightly ajar, you may be sure that this ancient enemy will kick it open with six-guns blazing. So don't leave it open. Don't give lust a foothold—or even a toehold.

— **Charles Swindoll**

November 2

Shout for joy, O heavens; rejoice, O earth; burst into song, O mountains! For the LORD comforts his people and will have compassion on his afflicted ones.
Isaiah 49:13

Passage for the Day: Isaiah 49:1–13

What was it that drew men to Jesus? Yes, he spoke with authority and he did miraculous and wonderful deeds, but I think the one thing that men could not ignore was the compassion and love that came from his heart and on to his face and into his words and deeds.

— Bob Benson

March 17

If a man marries a woman who becomes displeasing
to him because he finds something indecent about her,
and he writes her a certificate of divorce,
gives it to her and sends her from his house . . .
Deuteronomy 24:1

Passage for the Day: Deuteronomy 24:1–5

Jesus is more impatient with Jewish divorce practices than almost anything else. . . . [He believed strongly in marriage's permanence.] But watch Jesus, in John 4, deal with a woman who had been married and divorced five times each, and who, in this shameful condition, was now living with a man to whom she was not married. Jesus clearly believes that divorce is not the end of hope. He puts her back on the track of abundant life. So Jesus is not simply a "purist" who shoots the wounded. He believes that anybody in any tragic condition can be salvaged and brought to wholeness and health today.

— **Donald M. Joy**

November 1

While Jesus was having dinner at Matthew's house,
many tax collectors and "sinners" came
and ate with him and his disciples.
Matthew 9:10

Passage for the Day: Matthew 9:9–13

Matthew wrote, "When the Pharisees saw this, they asked his disciples, 'Why does your teacher eat with tax collectors and "sinners"?' On hearing this, Jesus said, 'It is not the healthy who need a doctor, but the sick'" (Matthew 9:11–12). In essence, Jesus was saying, "My job here on earth is to get sinners back to God, not to worry about the good people."

— **Jim Conway**

March 18

"Therefore, I tell you, her many sins have been forgiven—for she loved much. But he who has been forgiven little loves little."
Luke 7:47

Passage for the Day: Luke 7:36–50

God has provided some beautiful resources to help us in our guilt. Church worship contains public or private confession and absolution. The Scriptures proclaim an accepting Lord who continually forgives people. This same Lord and Savior died for us in an ultimate act of forgiveness, and he rose to give us new life. He has given us the Lord's Supper to strengthen us and to reconcile us with God.

— **Philip W. Williams**

October 31

In this you greatly rejoice,
though now for a little while you may
have had to suffer grief in all kinds of trials.
1 Peter 1:6

Passage for the Day: 1 Peter 1:3–9

[God's] not the Cosmic Bookkeeper, the one to blame if things don't work out the way you think they should. Life isn't always fair, at least in the short run, but the Bible taught me not to confuse life with God. When you're confronted with trouble you don't ask, "Why me!" You ask God, "What do you want me to do in this situation?"

— **Dave Dravecky**

March 19

Dishonest money dwindles away, but
he who gathers money little by little makes it grow.
Proverbs 13:11

Passage for the Day: Proverbs 13:7–11

How do you achieve one or more of the long-term goals, such as financial independence, college education, improving your lifestyle, getting out of debt, making major contributions or starting your own business? The answer is simple—spend less than you earn and do it for a long time.

— **Ron Blue**

October 30

Who is he, this King of glory?
The LORD Almighty—he is the King of glory.
Psalm 24:10

Passage for the Day: Psalm 24:1–10

Christ is Lord of all of life. If he is not, if he only presides over what we do on Sunday or at home, if he is only an ideal, if Jesus is merely a name in a book we read to our children—then he really isn't our Lord at all. He doesn't really matter in what matters most to most of us: our work.

— Doug Sherman and
William Hendricks

March 20

All they asked was that we should continue to remember the poor, the very thing I was eager to do.
Galatians 2:10

Passage for the Day: Galatians 2:6–10

Scripture adds a purely benevolent purpose to work: to earn money in order to give it away to others. In fact, the overwhelming thrust of the Scriptures is that as God sees fit to prosper us, our abundance should begin to spill over and start benefiting others who, for a variety of reasons, are in need.

— **Doug Sherman and William Hendricks**

October 29

*This is what the L*ORD *says—he who made you,*
who formed you in the womb, and who will help you:
Do not be afraid, O Jacob, my servant,
Jeshurun, whom I have chosen.
Isaiah 44:2

Passage for the Day: Isaiah 44:1–5

No matter how difficult life becomes, we belong in families. There may be times when we let down those we love and fail people who care the most, but through it all we discover a group of people who make us feel that we belong, who say, "What happens to you matters to me." Thus we stand together and face all of life with a confidence born of a sure identity in the family.

— **John F. Westfall**

March 21

"Have I not commanded you? Be strong and courageous.
Do not be terrified; do not be discouraged, for the LORD
your God will be with you wherever you go."
Joshua 1:9

Passage for the Day: Joshua 1:1–11

God calls the laity to do a job the clergy cannot do in many instances. In a parish I once served, a close friend who was a doctor became quite ill. . . . One day I went to see this Christian doctor and found him greatly improved and free from fear. . . . He told me of a visit a few hours before with a senior surgeon in the area who had prayed with him and given him a prescription. The prescription was to read Joshua 1:9. My friend had been touched by God, and not through a clergyman but through a brother physician.

— Bruce Larson

October 28

To this John replied, "A man can receive only
what is given him from heaven."
John 3:27

Passage for the Day: John 3:27–29

What we think of God makes a tremendous difference in our lives. Where we get our ideas of God makes a tremendous difference too. We can gather up data and develop our own image of God, or we can allow God to reveal himself in a self-portrait—his Son, Jesus Christ.

— Reuben R. Welch

March 22

Then he said to them, "Watch out! Be on your guard against all kinds of greed; a man's life does not consist in the abundance of his possessions."
Luke 12:15

Passage for the Day: Luke 12:13–21

The caution in this verse is clear: "Beware, and be on your guard against *every form of greed*." Debt makes it very easy to fund greeds; yet in doing so, we may violate the Biblical principle set forth in this verse. The question to ask is, "Am I funding my *needs* or my *greeds*?"

— Ron Blue

October 27

Brothers, we do not want you to be ignorant about those who fall asleep, or to grieve like the rest of men, who have no hope.
1 Thessalonians 4:13

Passage for the Day: 1 Thessalonians 4:13–18

Christians, in company with all men, experience grief, but unlike others, Christians do not grieve as people without hope. The assurance of the resurrection and the trust in God's power to turn bad Fridays into Good Fridays keep grief from being overwhelming; but nonetheless, God gives no crowns to those who refuse to weep.

— **Haddon W. Robinson**

March 23

Stern discipline awaits him who leaves the path;
he who hates correction will die.
Proverbs 15:10

Passage for the Day: Proverbs 15:7–10

If we are not accountable to someone else, we may never understand why people reject our advice. We must learn to accept constructive criticism ourselves.

— Reggie White

October 26

So the next generation would know them,
even the children yet to be born,
and they in turn would tell their children.
Psalm 78:6

Passage for the Day: Psalm 78:1–8

      The choices that you make with your family today will determine the quality of life in your family tree for generations to come. That's why one man can make a difference. And if you save your boys, it will be the greatest and most fulfilling task of your life.

— Steve Farrar

March 24

And pray for us, too, that God may open a door
for our message, so that we may proclaim the mystery
of Christ, for which I am in chains.
Colossians 4:3

Passage for the Day: Colossians 4:2–6

We are walking witnesses for Jesus Christ wherever we go. How can we do less than witness with all our heart. Our styles may be different, but the intensity shouldn't be. I know all Christians can't do it in the same manner as I do, but I have no choice but to do it with all my heart.

— **Reggie White**

October 25

For God did not give us a spirit of timidity,
but a spirit of power, of love and of self-discipline.
2 Timothy 1:7

Passage for the Day: 2 Timothy 1:5–7

People know where I'm coming from without my having to harp on it all the time. I know that the message of Christ offends because it calls sin sin and says we are all sinners. There's no way to soften that truth. It's jarring and can alienate people until they begin to realize that it's true.

— **Orel Hershiser**

March 25

"But if serving the LORD seems undesirable to you, then choose for yourselves this day whom you will serve, whether the gods your forefathers served beyond the River, or the gods of the Amorites, in whose land you are living. But as for me and my household, we will serve the LORD."
Joshua 24:15

Passage for the Day: Joshua 24:14–24

Remedies for the miseries of marital diseases: . . . Reserve time for aloneness and allow neither children, in-laws, neighbors, church activities, pesky salesmen, or work brought home from the office to interfere. Take occasional honeymoons, be they only for a night, just to get away. . . .

Say with Joshua, "But as for me and my household, we will serve the Lord." Always worship together and serve together in the same church, and pray together at home.

— **A. Dudley Dennison**

October 24

*Hide your face from my sins
and blot out all my iniquity.*
Psalm 51:9

Passage for the Day: Psalm 51:1–12

It's hard for a perfectionist like me, but I have to admit I can never be good enough. No matter how sound my strategy, how much I study, how hard I work—I'll always be a failure when it comes to being perfect. Yet God loves me anyway. And believing that gives me the greatest sense of peace, calm and security in the world.

— Tom Landry

"I tell you, use worldly wealth to gain friends for yourselves, so that when it is gone, you will be welcomed into eternal dwellings."
Luke 16:9

Passage for the Day: Luke 16:1–13

Now neither Jesus nor the boss ever praised deceitfulness, dishonesty or creative bookkeeping. But both of them recognized the accountant's vision. When faced with a serious problem, he did not hide, blame somebody, run to the bottle or jump off a cliff. Instead, he faced his problem and came up with a shrewd way to solve it. Jesus commended him because, as soon as he saw his problem, he became solution oriented.

— **Bill Hybels**

October 23

For you yourselves know how you ought to follow our example. We were not idle when we were with you.
2 Thessalonians 3:7

Passage for the Day: 2 Thessalonians 3:6–15

Work in a normal, healthy human context, work with a sane and moderate human measure, integrated in a productive social milieu, is by itself capable of contributing much to the spiritual life. But work that is disordered, irrational, unproductive, dominated by the exhausting frenzies and wastefulness of a worldwide struggle for power and wealth, is not necessarily going to make a valid contribution to the spiritual lives of all those engaged in it.

— **Thomas Merton**

*"He will wipe every tear from their eyes. There will be no
more death or mourning or crying or pain, for
the old order of things has passed away."*
Revelation 21:4

Passage for the Day: Revelation 21:1–5

Oh yes, we mourn . . . But we also have hope—bright hope
for tomorrow, when all who trust in Jesus Christ as Savior will
move beyond pain and grief forever because we shall be forever with
the Lord. And it is not just some pipe dream, some opium to stupefy
and mislead hurting people. It is real, because Christ is real,
because in our past there is a blood-stained cross on which the
Prince of Glory died. Because of that bloody, pain-filled past we have
hope when all things are made new and death shall be no more, nor
grief, nor crying.

— **Gerald Oosterveen**

October 22

When the perishable has been clothed with the imperishable, and the mortal with immortality, then the saying that is written will come true: "Death has been swallowed up in victory."
1 Corinthians 15:54

Passage for the Day: 1 Corinthians 15:54–57

If sympathy for the world's wounds is not enlarged by our anguish, if love for those around us is not expanded, if gratitude for what is good does not flame up, if insight is not deepened, if commitment to what is important is not strengthened, if aching for a new day is not intensified, if hope is weakened and faith diminished, if from the experience of death comes nothing good, then death has won. Then death, be proud.

So I shall struggle to live the reality of Christ's rising and death's dying.

— **Nicholas Wolterstorff**

You became imitators of us and of the Lord;
in spite of severe suffering, you welcomed the message
with the joy given by the Holy Spirit.
1 Thessalonians 1:6

Passage for the Day: 1 Thessalonians 1:2–10

I don't mind being a role model. I'm flattered when people say they'd like their kids to be like me. To me, being a role model is a heavy responsibility and a gift from God. I accept it openheartedly. But at the same time, I don't feel I should become more important in a kid's life than his father and mother. Very few kids ever actually emulate their heroes. They do what their parents did. Parents are the most important role models in their children's lives, for good or bad.

— **Mike Singletary**

October 21

"But for you who revere my name,
the sun of righteousness will rise with healing
in its wings. And you will go out and leap like
calves released from the stall."
Malachi 4:2

Passage for the Day: Malachi 4:1–6

[The voices of the prophets] soar like songbirds' when the prophets turn at last to describe the Joy beyond the walls of the world. . . . One day, says Malachi, we will leap like calves released from the stall. There will be no fear then, and no pain. No infants will die; no tears will fall. Among the nations, peace will flow like a river, and armies will melt their weapons into farm tools. No one will complain about the hiddenness of God in that day. His glory will fill the earth, and the sun will seem dim by contrast.

— **Philip Yancey**

March 29

*Then she called, "Samson, the Philistines
are upon you!" He awoke from his sleep and thought,
"I'll go out as before and shake myself free."
But he did not know that the LORD had left him.*
Judges 16:20

Passage for the Day: Judges 16:4–22

Samson's tragic fall led to the end of his freedom. He was a prisoner of the Philistines, a sorry figure they used for entertainment. . . . [Aristotle] said tragedy should lead to a *catharsis* in those who truly understand what has gone on. . . . Having seen a great person fall, people should be cleansed of their own pride, Aristotle wrote. They should see themselves in the great fall of a tragic hero. That's something for all of us to think about when we're patting ourselves on the back and taking the credit . . . instead of giving it to God.

— **James C. Schaap**

"What is it you want?" he asked.

**She said, *"Grant that one of these two sons
of mine may sit at your right and
the other at your left in your kingdom."***
Matthew 20:21

Passage for the Day: Matthew 20:20–28

What makes the temptation of power so seemingly
irresistible? Maybe it is that power offers an easy substitute for the
hard task of love. It seems easier to be God than to love God, easier
to control people than to love people, easier to own life than to love
life.

— **Henri Nouwen**

March 30

When Jesus heard this, he said to him, "You still lack one thing. Sell everything you have and give to the poor, and you will have treasure in heaven. Then come, follow me."
Luke 18:22

Passage for the Day: Luke 18:18–30

[Missionaries are asked regularly to share their belongings with those around them.] Before worrying ourselves over how many shirts to give and how many to keep, we should make sure we are in a place where we can hear what God is saying to us and that we would be willing to "sell everything" if he told us to. If we have really died to self and aren't just kidding ourselves, and if the compassion of Christ is discernible in our lives, then the number of shirts we give and keep is no longer so important, and the barriers created by our wealth largely disappear.

— **Thomas Hale**

October 19

My dear brothers, take note of this:
Everyone should be quick to listen,
slow to speak and slow to become angry.
James 1:19

Passage for the Day: James 1:19–21

The world aches for good listeners. Many doctors report that they daily see patients who have nothing physically wrong with them. They merely need someone to listen to them.

— **William E. Diehl**

March 31

A little sleep, a little slumber,
a little folding of the hands to rest . . .
Proverbs 24:33

Passage for the Day: Proverbs 24:33–34

If we act like tourists or sluggards when it comes to building value into our children, heartache may enter our homes as stealthily as a prowler, or discouragement may burst upon us as forcefully as an armed man.

No matter how old your children are, it's never too late to unfold your hands and start honoring them. When you consistently apply this concept, you save them the heartache of damaged relationships, and you also give them the foundation they will need to truly value God, themselves and others.

— **Gary Smalley and John Trent**

October 18

*She had a sister called Mary,
who sat at the Lord's feet
listening to what he said.*
Luke 10:39

Passage for the Day: Luke 10:38–42

Thank you for the privilege of sitting at those nail-scarred feet. Grant me the grace never to regard that privilege casually, nor to neglect it, but to come there humbly, and come there often . . . because you are worthy to be adored, O beautiful Savior . . . because you are worthy to be adored.

— Ken Gire

April 1

It is God's will that you should be sanctified:
that you should avoid sexual immorality.
1 Thessalonians 4:3

Passage for the Day: 1 Thessalonians 4:3–8

What I am recommending to my unmarried readers is this: *stay out of bed unless you go there alone!* Not only is virginity the only way to avoid disease, it is also the best foundation for a healthy marriage. That's the way the system was designed by the Creator and no one has yet devised a way to improve on his plan.

— **James Dobson**

October 17

For the love of money is a root of all kinds of evil.
Some people, eager for money, have wandered from the
faith and pierced themselves with many griefs.
1 Timothy 6:10

Passage for the Day: 1 Timothy 6:7–10

Is money the root of all evil? No. The love of money is. But we shouldn't rest too easily because of that distinction. We show what we love by that to which we most happily devote our attention.

— Daniel Taylor

April 2

Just then Boaz arrived from Bethlehem and greeted the harvesters, "The LORD be with you!"

"The LORD bless you!" they called back.
Ruth 2:4

Passage for the Day: Ruth 2:1–4

The blessing which is appropriate for worship is appropriate also for the work place. Boaz's exchange of blessing with his workforce is very similar to that exchanged at the end of worship. There is no separation in the Old Testament between the "sacred" and the "secular": the whole of life is lived as "before the face of God."

— **David Atkinson**

October 16

What, then, shall we say in response to this?
If God is for us, who can be against us?
Romans 8:31

Passage for the Day: Romans 8:31–39

God is on our side, right or wrong, because even when we are wrong, he still loves us.

— Michael Card

April 3

"I will remain in the world no longer, but they are still in the world, and I am coming to you. Holy Father, protect them by the power of your name—the name you gave me—so that they may be one as we are one." John 17:11

Passage for the Day: John 17:6–12

How can any organism [the church] composed of such diversity attain even a semblance of unity? . . . I have seen my share of unlikely seekers after God. And I must admit that most of my worship in the last thirty years has not taken place among people who have shared my taste in music, speech, or even thought. But over those years I have been profoundly—and humbly—impressed that I find God in the faces of my fellow worshipers by sharing with people who are shockingly different from each other and from me.

— **Paul Brand**

October 15

There will always be poor people in the land.
Therefore I command you to be openhanded toward
your brothers and toward the poor
and needy in your land.
Deuteronomy 15:11

Passage for the Day: Deuteronomy 15:7–11

The by-product of modern technocracy is the loss of our sense of caring and awareness of one another. But if we Christians get out of our pews, seek justice, do the Word of God and lift up Christ, we will see that sense of community restored.

— **Charles Colson**

April 4

All his days his work is pain and grief;
even at night his mind does not rest.
This too is meaningless.
Ecclesiastes 2:23

Passage for the Day: Ecclesiastes 2:17–26

The accelerated pace of modern living tends to rob us of natural recovery time, so that must be planned into our lives by deliberate design. Even Jesus was aware of this need for recovery. In Mark 6:31, he told his disciples, "Come with me by yourselves to a quiet place and get some rest."

If Jesus thought it necessary for him and his disciples to rest from time to time, who are we to think we can get by without it?

— **Archibald Hart**

October 14

Sitting down, Jesus called the Twelve and said,
"If anyone wants to be first, he must be the very last,
and the servant of all."
Mark 9:35

Passage for the Day: Mark 9:33–37

A home is . . . filled with fragrant and appealing spiritual riches when each member adopts a servant's spirit. Most family arguments and dissension stem from a failure to yield personal rights. A person filled with the Spirit of Christ strongly desires to serve. He does not seek to establish his own emotional turf but freely edifies and encourages other family members through his servant spirit.

— **Charles Stanley**

April 5

Pray continually.
1 Thessalonians 5:17

Passage for the Day: 1 Thessalonians 5:16–18

God never promised to tell me why everything happens the way it does. But he did promise me that anytime I wanted to talk, he would be happy to listen. And in a world where so many people feel they are all alone, that's a pretty great thing to know.

One more thing. God not only listens, he talks too. So when you are praying, *keep your ears open!*

— **Daniel Taylor**

October 13

The LORD is slow to anger and great in power; the LORD will not leave the guilty unpunished. His way is in the whirlwind and storm, and clouds are the dust of his feet.
Nahum 1:3

Passage for the Day: Nahum 1:2–6

Until the evil man finds evil unmistakably present in his existence, in the form of pain, he is enclosed in illusion. . . . No doubt Pain as God's megaphone is a terrible instrument; it may lead to final and unrepented rebellion. But it gives the only opportunity the bad man can have for amendment. It removes the veil; it plants the flag of truth within the fortress of a rebel soul.

— C.S. Lewis

April 6

He raises the poor from the dust and lifts the needy from the ash heap; he seats them with princes and has them inherit a throne of honor. "For the foundations of the earth are the LORD's; upon them he has set the world."
1 Samuel 2:8

Passage for the Day: 1 Samuel 2:6–10

We all are poor in some way or other. The person who thinks money is the measure of success suffers from a kind of poverty of the imagination and intellect as well as of the spirit. Others suffer a kind of poverty of the emotions, unable to intertwine their lives affirmingly with the lives of others. And the Bible tells us we are all poor before God. God offers us all of creation and a relationship with him and we have only our brokenness to offer back. (Thankfully, that is all that he requires.)

— **Daniel Taylor**

October 12

*Fathers, do not exasperate your children; instead, bring
them up in the training and instruction of the Lord.
Ephesians 6:4*

Passage for the Day: Ephesians 6:1–4

Experience has shown us that the men who are happiest
and most content in the masculine role today are those whose
fathers invested a great deal of time and energy in their lives. These
dads . . . were committed to maintaining a positive, nurturing
relationship with their sons. These fathers supported their sons in
their chosen careers, attempted to understand their ambitions (even
when they differed from their own), and appreciated their
achievements. As a result of their investment, their sons are among
the most well-adjusted and peaceful husbands and fathers in our
society.

— **Stephen Arterburn
and David Stoop**

April 7

*To those who sold doves he said, "Get these out of here!
How dare you turn my Father's house into a market!"*
John 2:16

Passage for the Day: John 2:13–17

Jesus didn't suppress his anger any more than he exploded
with rage that day in the temple. His anger was up front, out in the
open. He responded to the situation quickly, positively and
appropriately, then went on with his business.

If a man buries his anger inside, he's only storing up
pressure for a later implosion (hurting himself) and/or explosion
(hurting others). If he doesn't bring his anger to the surface and deal
with it, someday, somewhere, somehow it will express itself in an
out-of-bounds manner, and somebody will get hurt.

— **Stephen Arterburn
and David Stoop**

October 11

"I have told you these things,
so that in me you may have peace.
In this world you will have trouble.
But take heart! I have overcome the world."
John 16:33

Passage for the Day: John 16:17–33

Grief is lessened when we have an eternal center for our lives. The good news of the Bible is simply this: men and women may have a relationship with the eternal God through faith in Jesus Christ. Putting it another way, Jesus Christ himself may become the hub of our entire life.

— **Haddon W. Robinson**

April 8

He has made everything beautiful in its time. He has also set eternity in the hearts of men; yet they cannot fathom what God has done from beginning to end.
Ecclesiastes 3:11

Passage for the Day: Ecclesiastes 3:9–22

A man's ultimate desire is for immortality.... That's part of what we mean when we say we want to be significant.... If we do not ultimately find our significance in Christ, then we will not survive the threshold between this world and the next. Our highest hopes will come to a screeching halt. It would be better if we had never been born.

— **Patrick Morley**

October 10

But the pot he was shaping from the clay was marred in his hands; so the potter formed it into another pot, shaping it as seemed best to him.
Jeremiah 18:4

Passage for the Day: Jeremiah 18:1–6

The potter has re-creative power. Jeremiah says that sometimes the pot is marred in the potter's hand. Sometimes the pot does not do what it was designed to do. But the potter just takes it and breaks it and molds it and makes it what he would have it to be. I'm glad to know that when I'm marred and broken, the Lord is not through with me yet. I want him to re-create me.

— **H. Beecher Hicks**

With this in mind, we constantly pray for you, that our God may count you worthy of his calling, and that by his power he may fulfill every good purpose of yours and every act prompted by your faith.
2 Thessalonians 1:11

Passage for the Day: 2 Thessalonians 1:3–12

We can speak of a man's choosing his vocation, but perhaps it is at least as accurate to speak of a vocation's choosing the man, of a call's being given and a man's hearing it, or not hearing it. And maybe that is the place to start: the business of listening and hearing. A man's life is full of all sorts of voices calling him in all sorts of directions. . . . The more alive and alert we are, the more clamorous our lives are. Which do we listen to? What kind of voice do we listen for?

— **Frederick Buechner**

October 9

Who is a God like you, who pardons sin and forgives the transgression of the remnant of his inheritance? You do not stay angry forever but delight to show mercy.
Micah 7:18

Passage for the Day: Micah 7:16–20

If God was willing to move quickly to restore fellowship with Adam and Eve [see Genesis 3:21], does it make sense that he would move any less quickly to restore fellowship with us? And if the heavenly Father was willing to move quickly to restore fellowship with sinners, how much more quickly should we move to restore fellowship with those who have wronged us?

— **Charles Stanley**

April 10

*Jesus said, "Father, forgive them, for they
do not know what they are doing."
And they divided up his clothes by casting lots.*
Luke 23:34

Passage for the Day: Luke 23:32–43

It's more than interesting to notice how unblemished
humanity responds to aloneness and mistreatment. As our Lord
hung on the cross, he didn't require others to treat him fairly. Even
though he was alone and wrongly treated beyond imagination and
even though he mightily wished his pain could be avoided, his
commitment to the Father's purpose and to rescuing us from
judgment never became secondary to his desire for immediate relief.
It would never have occurred to him to use suffering to excuse self-
interest.

— **Larry Crabb**

October 8

*For we brought nothing into the world, and
we can take nothing out of it.*
1 Timothy 6:7

Passage for the Day: 1 Timothy 6:3–10

Nothing prohibits Christians from obeying God more than the tug of material comforts. Once we have adjusted to a lifestyle that includes many comforts, it is very difficult to surrender them to serve God. Obviously, God doesn't call everyone to leave his vocation and go into what is traditionally called "Christian work." God can and does use Christians everywhere. But in order to be used by God in any capacity, a Christian must be willing to serve God no matter what the costs.

— **Larry Burkett**

April 11

After David had finished talking with Saul,
Jonathan became one in spirit with David,
and he loved him as himself.
1 Samuel 18:1

Passage for the Day: 1 Samuel 18:1–4

To show outwardly his inward love, Jonathan took off his
robe, tunic, sword, bow and belt and gave them all to his dear friend,
David. This symbolic gesture, this outward expression of Jonathan's
love, affected greatly their commitment to each other. . . . It is vital
that friends know that we care about them personally. The very
least we can do is tell them how highly we value them and our
relationship with them. In short, we should form covenants with
friends.

— **David W. Smith**

October 7

But you are a chosen people, a royal priesthood,
a holy nation, a people belonging to God, that you may
declare the praises of him who called you out
of darkness into his wonderful light.
1 Peter 2:9

Passage for the Day: 1 Peter 2:9–12

Let what you do arise out of who you are. Being is more important than doing. As for me, I have decided that whatever I do for the rest of my life, it will not be in order to have an identity. It will be the result of allowing my God-given self to emerge. I'm done with posturing for a public that demands an unattainable and hypocritical perfection.

— **Stan Mooneyham**

April 12

In reply Jesus declared,
"I tell you the truth, no one can see
the kingdom of God unless
he is born again."
John 3:3

Passage for the Day: John 3:3–6

If you've invited Christ into your life, you have been reborn and the Holy Spirit is working to help you become all that God wants you to be.

— **Jim Conway**

October 6

Hate evil, love good; maintain justice in the courts.
Perhaps the LORD God Almighty will have mercy
on the remnant of Joseph.
Amos 5:15

Passage for the Day: Amos 5:11–17

After 10 years in a Soviet gulag, Alexander Solzhenitsyn wrote "Bless you, prison, for having been in my life." For it was there he learned that "the meaning of earthly existence lies, not as we have grown used to thinking, in prospering, but in the development of the soul." I too can say, "Bless you, prison," for it was there that I learned to see justice in the way that Amos and Micah and Jeremiah and Isaiah saw it.

— **Charles Colson**

April 13

Guard your steps when you go to the house of God.
Go near to listen rather than to offer the sacrifice of
fools, who do not know that they do wrong.
Ecclesiastes 5:1

Passage for the Day: Ecclesiastes 5:1–7

For the man or woman who comes to know and love God as Father in such intimacy, the times of solitude are the most exquisite in all of life. They are *"a rendezvous with the Beloved."* They are anticipated eagerly; awaited with acute expectancy; relished with enthusiasm. In a word, these times are highlights of life.

— **W. Phillip Keller**

October 5

Not only so, but we also rejoice in our sufferings,
because we know that suffering produces perseverance.
Romans 5:3

Passage for the Day: Romans 5:1–11

Calmly comforting [your children] at the beginning of a
trial lays the foundation for them to find value in their experience.
Calmness comes from within us when we are confident in God's
Word. Painful trials produce maturity, which leads to love!

— **Gary Smalley and**
John Trent

April 14

For even when we were with you,
we gave you this rule:
"If a man will not work, he shall not eat."
2 Thessalonians 3:10

Passage for the Day: 2 Thessalonians 3:6–15

The spiritual life is not a life of quiet withdrawal, a hothouse of growth of artificial ascetic practices beyond the reach of people living ordinary lives. It is in the ordinary duties and labors of life that the Christian can and should develop his spiritual union with God.

— **Thomas Merton**

October 4

*I led them with cords of human kindness,
with ties of love; I lifted the yoke from
their neck and bent down to feed them.
Hosea 11:4*

Passage for the Day: Hosea 11:1–11

When I was still a wayward young man, far removed from
God, he pursued me in loving concern down the tangled paths of my
escapades. He did not give up on me; he did not write me off. He did
not despise, reject or abandon me. Instead, he followed me faithfully
out into the deep darkness and despair of my lonely wanderings.

Only Christ, my Friend, could possibly care enough to draw
me to himself, to bring me back gently to my Father, to patiently lay
down his life for me that I might come to know him.

— **W. Phillip Keller**

April 15

Not so with you. Instead, whoever wants to become
great among you must be your servant.
Mark 10:43

Passage for the Day: Mark 10:35–45

The Christian . . . may or may not have more than his
neighbor, but that does not distinguish him. What does distinguish
the Christian from the world is the absence of any anxiety, which
might have come as a result of the loss of something he has
managed or even God's denial of something he wants. Why? Because
the Christian's treasure is not on earth. The world and its temporal
toys do not possess him. He is prayerful, but not the least bit
anxious about the tremendous uncertainty facing our national and
world economy.

— **Ron Blue**

October 3

Do not be deceived: God cannot be mocked.
A man reaps what he sows.
Galatians 6:7

Passage for the Day: Galatians 6:7–8

Giving and gratitude go together like humor and laughter, like having one's back rubbed and the sigh that follows, like a blowing wind and the murmur of wind chimes. Gratitude keeps alive the rhythm or grace given and grace grateful, a lively lilt that lightens a heavy world.

— Lewis B. Smedes

April 16

Jonathan spoke well of David to Saul his father and said to him, "Let not the king do wrong to his servant David; he has not wronged you, and what he has done has benefited you greatly."
1 Samuel 19:4

Passage for the Day: 1 Samuel 19:1–7

If you study the friendship between David and Jonathan, you will walk away with a good understanding of what a healthy friendship between men can and should be like. . . . I would say that any definition should include the following:

* Unconditional love   * Personal enjoyment
* Mutual acceptance   * Mutual interests
* Mutual commitment   * Mutual loyalty

In short, friendship involves a concern for and involvement with the well-being of another.

— **David W. Smith**

October 2

But they urged him strongly, "Stay with us,
for it is nearly evening; the day is almost over."
So he went in to stay with them.
Luke 24:29

Passage for the Day: Luke 24:28–35

[God] is with us on our journeys. He is there when we are home. He sits with us at our table. He knows about funerals and weddings and commencements and hospitals and jails and unemployment and labor and laughter and rest and tears. He knows because he is with us. He comes to us again and again.

— **Bob Benson**

April 17

After he said this,
he showed them his hands and side.
The disciples were overjoyed
when they saw the Lord.
John 20:20

Passage for the Day: John 20:19–23

As Jesus' resurrected body was recognized by its scars, so his body, the church, should be known by its scars and tears and the unspeakable joy it knows in spite of, and indeed because of, it all.

— **Michael Card**

October 1

Know therefore that the L ORD your God is God;
he is the faithful God, keeping his covenant
of love to a thousand generations of those
who love him and keep his commands.
Deuteronomy 7:9

Passage for the Day: Deuteronomy 7:9–11

For me, the good news is that the great One who is totally
other and past finding out has humbled himself and presented
himself to us not in power but in love.

— **Tony Campolo**

April 18

Let him kiss me with the kisses of his mouth—
for your love is more delightful than wine.
Song of Songs 1:2

Passage for the Day: Song of Songs 1:1–4

No wonder the Creator made marriage permanent—after a lifetime we have only just begun to understand the marvelous inner clockwork of each other.

— Richard Foster

September 30

"No one knows about that day or hour, not even the angels in heaven, nor the Son, but only the Father."
Mark 13:32

Passage for the Day: Mark 13:32–37

The expectation of Jesus' coming provides a goal that shapes and unifies life in accordance with its origins in Christ, in patterns that are consonate with its completion in Christ. This urgency is liberating, for it compels us to stay awake, deeply and earnestly aware of who we are and what we are doing, keeping us free from trivia that . . . can make prisoners of us as effectively as any ball and chain.

— **Eugene H. Peterson**

April 19

Here is a trustworthy saying that deserves full acceptance: Christ Jesus came into the world to save sinners—of whom I am the worst.
1 Timothy 1:15

Passage for the Day: 1 Timothy 1:12–17

God loves unconditionally. God doesn't withhold love until we arrive at perfection. He loves us while we are growing and even while we are his enemies. His love enables us to change and mature.
— Jim Conway

September 29

What is more, I consider everything a loss compared to the surpassing greatness of knowing Christ Jesus my Lord, for whose sake I have lost all things. I consider them rubbish, that I may gain Christ.
Philippians 3:8

Passage for the Day: Philippians 3:7–11

You can learn about God with your mind or through your experience. God prefers the latter. He wants us to know him experientially, to engage him with our whole lives.

— John Timmer

April 20

My dear children, for whom I am again in the pains of childbirth until Christ is formed in you . . .
Galatians 4:19

Passage for the Day: Galatians 4:12–20

Marriage partners tend to become like each other, taking on the other's qualities, or developing the opposite characteristics in negative reaction to the other.

Leadership shared in mutual respect can establish a climate of dignity, freedom and responsibility, creating an atmosphere which is both comforting and stimulating to both—a Christian atmosphere. In it, each is free to grow toward personal maturity and each is eager to see the shape of Christ forming in the other.

— **David Augsburger**

September 28

*O Israel, put your hope in the L*ORD*, for with the L*ORD *is unfailing love and with him is full redemption.*
Psalm 130:7

Passage for the Day: Psalm 130:1–8

True prayer is an encounter with the Holy in which we realize not only our creatureliness and guilt but also the joy of knowing that our sins are forgiven through the atoning death of the divine Savior, Jesus Christ. In such an encounter, we are impelled not only to bow before God and seek his mercy but also to offer thanksgiving for grace that goes out to undeserving sinners.

— Donald Bloesch

***Then David said to Nathan,
"I have sinned against the LORD."***

***Nathan replied, "The LORD has taken away your sin.
You are not going to die."***
2 Samuel 12:13

Passage for the Day: 2 Samuel 11:1–27

Ever read the Bible about David's moral wreck? I call it Bathshebagate. It involved hanky-panky, adultery, and even the murder of Bathsheba's husband. . . . David was exposed. His past righteousness and achievement were nullified.

But now read Psalm 51. David did the only thing you can do when you're caught red-handed. He confessed and asked for a new heart to replace the old one . . . a spiritual and moral transplant. . . . You can begin again after moral failure.

— Gerald Mann

September 27

Dear friends, do not be surprised at the painful trial you are suffering, as though something strange were happening to you.
1 Peter 4:12

Passage for the Day: 1 Peter 4:12–13

It's hard to understand . . . suffering . . . I told her [a woman whose husband had cancer], but this much I did know: You can't blame God for it. Sooner or later our life on this earth is going to pass. Even the best lives someday come to an end. The only thing that will matter then is whether or not we'll get to heaven. I believe in miracles, that God can and does heal people, but more important than that, I believe in the eternal hope of heaven. When I die, that's where I'm going, because heaven is my home.

— **Dave Dravecky**

April 22

"He must become greater;
I must become less."
John 3:30

Passage for the Day: John 3:22–36

There is nothing phony about John's humility—it's real. He has come to grips with who he really is in relation to Jesus. A humble man is not afraid to admit it. Such a man admits openly, "I must go on decreasing. He must go on increasing."

— **D. Stuart Briscoe**

September 26

LORD, I have heard of your fame; I stand in awe of your deeds, O LORD. Renew them in our day, in our time make them known; in wrath remember mercy.
Habakkuk 3:2

Passage for the Day: Habakkuk 3:1–19

Praying means giving up a false security, no longer looking for arguments which will protect you if you get pushed into a corner, no longer setting your hope on a couple of lighter moments which your life might still offer. Praying means to stop expecting from God that same small-mindedness which you discover in yourself. To pray is to walk in the full light of God, and to say simply, without holding back, "I am a man and you are God."

— **Henri Nouwen**

April 23

*My lover spoke and said to me, "Arise, my darling, my
beautiful one, and come with me."*
Song of Songs 2:10

Passage for the Day: Song of Songs 2:3–13

Fidelity means a stubborn dedication to growth in personal
relationship. A marriage partnership must have room for individual
growth; but at the beating heart of any marriage is the delicate,
fragile—often painful—but potentially joyful relationship of two
persons face to face in personal encounter.

— **Lewis B. Smedes**

September 25

But the fruit of the Spirit is love, joy, peace, patience,
kindness, goodness, faithfulness . . .
Galatians 5:22

Passage for the Day: Galatians 5:22–23

Our goal is balance . . . always balance. Not either-or, but both-and. Not just *tough*. That alone makes a man cold, distant, intolerant, unbearable. But tough *and* tender . . . gentle, thoughtful, teachable, considerate.

— Charles Swindoll

April 24

If anyone does not provide for his relatives, and especially for his immediate family, he has denied the faith and is worse than an unbeliever.
1 Timothy 5:8

Passage for the Day: 1 Timothy 5:1–8

This is remarkably strong language! Failing to try to meet even the basic needs of one's family is denying the faith. Why? Because it directly opposes God's command to love those who are our own. In fact, it is to act worse than an unbeliever, because even pagans have the sense and decency to provide a livelihood for their families.

— **Doug Sherman and William Hendricks**

September 24

*Remember those earlier days after you had received the
light, when you stood your ground in a great contest
in the face of suffering.*
Hebrews 10:32

Passage for the Day: Hebrews 10:32–39

Biblical principles are like powerful flashlights that can
light up even the darkest trial your children may experience.
Because you know this, you can verbally and nonverbally convey
this message to your children as they watch your response to their
trials. And you can also ask them if they are willing to look for what
God has to teach them in the difficulty they've experienced.

— **Gary Smalley and
John Trent**

April 25

"As for God, his way is perfect; the word of the L<small>ORD</small> is flawless. He is a shield for all who take refuge in him."
2 Samuel 22:31

Passage for the Day: 2 Samuel 22:31–51

This is the longing of all mankind—to have security, to know where one's place is. God created man and then he created a place for him, the Garden of Eden. When man lost God, he lost at the same time his place. Since then, the longing for a place where he belongs, where he feels at home, is in the heart of every human being. . . . In light of this, Jesus' promise "to prepare a place" for us is filled with new meaning (John 14:2). Those who have found him have found their place.

— **Walter Trobisch**

September 23

"Who among the gods is like you, O LORD?
Who is like you—majestic in holiness,
awesome in glory, working wonders?"
Exodus 15:11

Passage for the Day: Exodus 15:11–18

     The most portentous fact about any person is not what he at any given time may say or do, but what he in his deep heart conceives God to be like. . . . A right conception of God is basic to practical Christian living. There is scarcely an error in doctrine or a failure in applying Christian ethics that cannot be traced finally to imperfect and ignoble thoughts about God.

— A.W. Tozer

April 26

*On the last and greatest day of the Feast,
Jesus stood and said in a loud voice, "If anyone is
thirsty, let him come to me and drink."*
John 7:37

Passage for the Day: John 7:37–44

The thirsty come. A ragged lot we are, bound together by broken dreams and collapsed promises. Fortunes that were never made. Families that were never built. Promises that were never kept. . . . We're thirsty for a clean conscience. We crave a clean slate. We yearn for a fresh start. We pray for a hand which will enter the dark cavern of our world and do for us the one thing we can't do for ourselves—make us right again.

— **Max Lucado**

September 22

*But those who hope in the L*ORD *will renew their
strength. They will soar on wings like eagles;
they will run and not grow weary,
they will walk and not be faint.
Isaiah 40:31*

Passage for the Day: Isaiah 40:18–31

It was Jesus himself who reminded us that we were to call
him Father—"Abba Father"—which is a lot more like calling him
Dad. I think Jesus was telling us that our Father is the one in the
stands who is standing on the seat, waving his coat in a circle over
his head, with tears of pride and happiness running down his face.

— **Bob Benson**

April 27

*He gives strength to the weary and
increases the power of the weak.
Isaiah 40:29*

Passage for the Day: Isaiah 40:27–31

Whenever there is the experience of weariness or
degradation, you may be certain you have done one of two things—
either you have disregarded a law of nature, or you have
deliberately got out of touch with God.

— Oswald Chambers

September 21

Has not the LORD made them one? In flesh and spirit they are his. And why one? Because he was seeking godly offspring. So guard yourself in your spirit, and do not break faith with the wife of your youth.
Malachi 2:15

Passage for the Day: Malachi 2:13–16

What will you do . . . when unexpected tornadoes blow through your home, or when the doldrums leave your sails sagging and silent? Will you pack it in and go home to Mama? Or will you pout and cry and seek ways to strike back? Or will your commitment hold you steady? These questions must be addressed *now*, before Satan has an opportunity to put his noose of discouragement around your neck. Set your jaw and clench your fists. Nothing short of death must ever be permitted to come between the two of you. *Nothing!*

— **James Dobson**

Fight the good fight of the faith.
Take hold of the eternal life
to which you were called when you made
your good confession in the presence
of many witnesses.
1 Timothy 6:12

Passage for the Day: 1 Timothy 6:11–16

To call myself a Christian and then not strive to be the best I can be and do the most I can with what has been given me would be the height of hypocrisy. Being a Christian is no excuse for mediocrity or passive acceptance of defeat. If anything, Christianity demands a higher standard, more devotion to the task.

— **Orel Hershiser**

September 20

*"My command is this: Love each other
as I have loved you."
John 15:12*

Passage for the Day: John 15:9–17

Christ called out in profound pathos—while the iron spikes tore through his hands and his feet—*"Father, forgive them, for they do not know what they are doing"* [Luke 23:34, italics added]. It was the intense heart-cry of our compassionate, caring God giving us himself, sharing with us his own life, in a superb act of selfless self-sacrifice.

— W. Phillip Keller

And said, "O LORD, God of Israel,
there is no God like you in heaven above
or on earth below—you who keep your covenant
of love with your servants who
continue wholeheartedly in your way."
1 Kings 8:23

Passage for the Day: 1 Kings 8:22–53

[Solomon's] prayer of dedication for the temple in 1 Kings 8 is one of the most majestic ever prayed. Yet by the end of his reign Solomon had squandered away nearly every advantage. . . . Success . . . seemed to eliminate Solomon's desire for God at all. The more he enjoyed the world's good gifts, the less he thought about the Giver.

— **Philip Yancey**

September 19

Let us not become weary in doing good,
for at the proper time we will reap a harvest
if we do not give up.
Galatians 6:9

Passage for the Day: Galatians 6:9–10

Persistent, faithful, plodding belief and hope are necessary if we are to remain free to give. Despair, which descends by dungeon steps to depression, is one of the major afflictions in our society. People seek relief from it sometimes in entertainment, sometimes in violence. Christians make their way out of it step by step, sometimes with great effort, on hardly visible footholds of sharing. The besetting temptation of the life of the Spirit is simply to quit.

— **Eugene H. Peterson**

April 30

So if the Son sets you free,
you will be free indeed.
John 8:36

Passage for the Day: John 8:32–41

The carpenter-preacher had said that he could by his death on a cross make people free of their guilt. He had been so credible in other things, I tried him on this one and found he delivered. The same forgiveness he extended to his executioners, he now handed me. My lifelong quest for truth and meaning has truly been met. I have been literally saved by his life.

— **Mark Ritchie**

September 18

*"The servant's master took pity on him,
canceled the debt and let him go."*
Matthew 18:27

Passage for the Day: Matthew 18:21–35

Forgiving is love's revolution against love's unfairness.
When we forgive, we ignore the normal laws that strap us to the
natural law of getting even and, by the alchemy of love, we release
ourselves from our own painful pasts.

— **Lewis B. Smedes**

May 1

*This is what the Sovereign LᵪRD, the
Holy One of Israel, says: "In repentance and rest is
your salvation, in quietness and trust is
your strength, but you would have none of it."
Isaiah 30:15*

Passage for the Day: Isaiah 30:15–18

This is the problem: People in a hurry never have time for recovery. Their minds have little time to meditate and pray so that problems can be put in perspective. In short, people in our age are showing signs of physiological disintegration because we are living at a pace that is too fast for our bodies.

— Archibald Hart

September 17

*"Be still before the LORD, all mankind,
because he has roused himself
from his holy dwelling."*
Zechariah 2:13

Passage for the Day: Zechariah 2:10–13

When the Holy Spirit is permitted to exercise his full sway in a redeemed heart there will likely be voluble praise first; then, when the crescendo rises beyond the ability of studied speech to express, comes song. When song breaks down under the weight of glory, then comes silence where the soul, held in deep fascination, feels itself blessed with an unutterable beatitude!

— **A. W. Tozer**

May 2

So do not be ashamed to testify about our Lord, or ashamed of me his prisoner. But join with me in suffering for the gospel, by the power of God.
2 Timothy 1:8

Passage for the Day: 2 Timothy 1:8–12

We're far from perfect. We fail. There are people who may think we are insincere or who think we're judgmental. I can't defend myself against people who say I'm phony. Only my family, true friends and I know who I really am inside. I'll have to answer for that someday. I can only do and be what I think God wants me to do and be. I never want to embarrass him or bring him shame.

— **Orel Hershiser**

September 16

I know what it is to be in need, and I know what it is to have plenty. I have learned the secret of being content in any and every situation, whether well fed or hungry, whether living in plenty or in want.
Philippians 4:12

Passage for the Day: Philippians 4:10–20.

It is important to grasp the truth that there is no shame in neediness. For those of us who were raised to appear strong, neediness is a horrible condition from which we turn away. . . . This may . . . inhibit our pursuing the very things we need most in life: relationships in which we are known intimately, in which we share vulnerably, and in which we discover love and accountability.

— John F. Westfall

May 3

*"For this is what the LORD, the God of Israel, says:
'The jar of flour will not be used up and the jug of oil
will not run dry until the day the
LORD gives rain on the land.'"*
1 Kings 17:14

Passage for the Day: 1 Kings 17:7–16

For the first time in my life I truly grasped the meaning of the hardship my mother lived under. No matter how often I looked at the income and compared it with what we had to pay out, it amazed me that my mother had kept [my brother] Curtis and me alive. And she did it with such style that our neighbors were convinced we were financially well off.

"You must be a financial wizard," I said.

"With God advising me," she said and laughed, "I sure am!"

— **Ben Carson**

September 15

Brothers, do not slander one another. Anyone who speaks against his brother or judges him speaks against the law and judges it. When you judge the law, you are not keeping it, but sitting in judgment on it.
James 4:11

Passage for the Day: James 4:7–12

More than anything else in heaven or on earth,
I pray for the power to love my fellow person,
to break through the damning bigotry,
the crippling prejudice,
the stifling self-centeredness
that smothers God's Spirit within me,
and to channel and communicate divine love
to lonely, loveless people about me.

— **Leslie Brandt**

May 4

*The thief comes only to steal
and kill and destroy;
I have come that they may
have life, and have it to the full.*
John 10:10

Passage for the Day: John 10:1–10

Although man can gain momentary happiness on the
mental, emotional or physical planes of life, he will never attain
lasting happiness as long as the God-void in his spiritual nature is
unfulfilled. He will never know abiding joy or have power to control
those weaker parts of his nature.

— **Tim LaHaye**

September 14

*"Is it a time for you yourselves to be living in your
paneled houses, while this house remains a ruin?"*
Haggai 1:4

Passage for the Day: Haggai 1:1–11

Men often have a distorted order of priorities. Physical
things are more important than relationships. Status is obtained by
the acquisition of material wealth rather than, say, the number of
close friends. . . . This distortion of emphasis on the material is
certainly not a recent development. The Old Testament prophet
Haggai, for example, warned that we are more concerned about
living in paneled houses *(material)* than we are about our
relationship with God and our fellowman *(immaterial)*.
— **David W. Smith**

May 5

*The plans of the diligent
lead to profit as surely as
haste leads to poverty.
Proverbs 21:5*

Passage for the Day: Proverbs 21:5–6

I feel it is so important to apply the rule that a husband and wife have perfect unity on their debt decisions. God has granted to women a special sense, which some have called intuition, that cannot be explained, but in many cases, it has kept a husband from making a poor decision.

— Ron Blue

September 13

"Will the one who contends with the Almighty correct him? Let him who accuses God answer him!"
Job 40:2

Passage for the Day: Job 40:1–14

God cannot be controlled. And he would be within his rights to either ignore our attempts at control or simply push us and our petty little pretensions aside. But thanks be to God, he is not like that. Instead, out of his grace and mercy he periodically reminds us of the folly of our ways. And one way he has done this in my life is through my children.

— S.D. Gaede

May 6

. . . no longer a slave, but better than a slave, as a dear brother. He is very dear to me but even dearer to you, both as a man and as a brother in the Lord.
Philemon 16

Passage for the Day: Philemon 12–18

Whatever your situation, whatever has happened in your past, remember that you are the loser if you do not deal with an unforgiving spirit. And the people around you suffer, too.

— Charles Stanley

September 12

*For the foolishness of God is wiser
than man's wisdom, and the weakness
of God is stronger than man's strength.
1 Corinthians 1:25*

Passage for the Day: 1 Corinthians 1:20–31

When it comes right down to it Lord
I choose to be your failure
before anyone else's success.
Keep me from reneging
on my choice.

— **Joseph Bayly**

"Honor your father and your mother, so that you may live long in the land the LORD your God is giving you."
Exodus 20:12

Passage for the Day: Exodus 20:12–17

During my previous readings of this verse, I had stopped after the first five words. That seemed to say it. . . . But as I lingered over the words that day in my *Guideposts* office, the totality of the promise hit me. God was giving us more than a command; he was telling us *why* it is important to honor our parents . . . "that you may live long in the land the Lord your God is giving you."

A new thought here—that when we war with parents, reject parents or are indifferent to them we may be missing out on a special blessing.

— **Leonard LeSourd**

September 11

"That day will be a day of wrath, a day of distress and anguish, a day of trouble and ruin, a day of darkness and gloom, a day of clouds and blackness."
Zephaniah 1:15

Passage for the Day: Zephaniah 1:14–18

I have prayed against political tyranny and unfairness and injustice. I have prayed for a miracle, for proof of God's existence. But as I read the prophets' descriptions of the day when God finally will take off all the wraps, one prayer overwhelms all others: "God, I hope I'm not around then." God freely admits he is holding back his power, but he restrains himself for our benefit. For all scoffers who call for direct action from the heavens, the prophets have ominous advice: Just wait.

— Philip Yancey

May 8

Jesus wept.
John 11:35

Passage for the Day: John 11:32–37

In that incident, once and for all, Jesus refuted by his tears
the notion that "big boys don't cry." He who remains history's perfect
and complete man stood by a graveside and wept.

— Haddon W.
Robinson

September 10

The Word became flesh and made his dwelling among us. We have seen his glory, the glory of the One and Only, who came from the Father, full of grace and truth.
John 1:14

Passage for the Day: John 1:1–14

It is not objective proof of God's existence that we want but the experience of God's presence. That is the miracle we are really after, and that is also, I think, the miracle that we really get.

— **Frederick Buechner**

A wife of noble character who can find?
She is worth far more than rubies.
Proverbs 31:10

Passage for the Day: Proverbs 31:10–31

What most people don't realize is that something is as true in my family as it is in almost any man's family: What our wives do and have done is much more valuable in terms of eternity than anything we could ever do.

— **Joe Gibbs**

September 9

"The King will reply, 'I tell you the truth, whatever you did for one of the least of these brothers of mine, you did for me.'"
Matthew 25:40

Passage for the Day: Matthew 25:31–40

How is it to be explained—the very heart and mystery of the Christian faith? To soothe those battered old heads, to grasp those poor [leprous] stumps, to take in one's arms those children consigned to dustbins, because it is his head, as they are his stumps and his children, of whom he said that whosoever received one such child in his name received him.

— Malcolm Muggeridge

May 10

*Do your best to present yourself to God as one approved,
a workman who does not need to be ashamed and who
correctly handles the word of truth.*
2 Timothy 2:15

Passage for the Day: 2 Timothy 2:14–19

He knows me. How do I know? Because while he changed me from sinner to forgiven-sinner, he also realigned my motives. I still had the character and personality, but my mind was renewed because I now wanted to do what he wanted me to do.

— **Orel Hershiser**

September 8

*I know that everything God does will endure forever;
nothing can be added to it and nothing taken from it.
God does it so that men will revere him.*
Ecclesiastes 3:14

Passage for the Day: Ecclesiastes 3:9–14

If we complain of time and take such joy in the seemingly timeless moment, . . . it suggests that we were created for eternity. Not only are we harried by time, we seem unable, despite a thousand generations, to even get used to it. We are always amazed at it—how fast it goes, how slowly it goes, how much of it is gone? We aren't adapted to it, nor at home in it. If that is so, it may appear as a proof, or at least a powerful suggestion, that eternity exists and is our home.

— **Sheldon Vanauken**

May 11

And Elisha prayed, "O LORD, open his eyes so he may see." Then the LORD opened the servant's eyes, and he looked and saw the hills full of horses and chariots of fire all around Elisha.
2 Kings 6:17

Passage for the Day: 2 Kings 6:14–17

The angels minister to God's servants in time of hardship and danger.

— Billy Graham

September 7

*Hear the word of the LORD, you Israelites, because
the LORD has a charge to bring against you who live in
the land: "There is no faithfulness, no love, no
acknowledgment of God in the land."*
Hosea 4:1

Passage for the Day: Hosea 4:1–9

Modern love seems to need the freedom to leave, otherwise
it was confining and restricting. The freedom to leave absolutely
precluded security of any sort. It means that separation is an option
that could be employed on any problem—emotional, financial,
sexual, anything. . . . I compared that to the marriage commitment. . . . The comparison made me laugh. It's small wonder that
there is so much insecurity in these modern, enlightened
relationships. What [my wife and I] had was a statement of real
love. It was out of the power of that committed love that we found
the deepest emotional
security.

— **Mark Ritchie**

May 12

*Now that I, your Lord and Teacher,
have washed your feet, you also should
wash one another's feet.
John 13:14*

Passage for the Day: John 13:1–17

Our Lord did not tell the disciples how they were to do it: He simply says—"Do it." He is not questioning whether or not they can do it; he is saying that they must do what the mastery of his ruling shows them they should do.

— **Oswald Chambers**

September 6

*"You are worthy, our Lord and God, to receive glory and
honor and power, for you created all things, and
by your will they were created and have their being."
Revelation 4:11*

Passage for the Day: Revelation 4:1–11

I long to give glory, honor and thanks to you always. May
your indwelling Spirit—the Spirit of glory—ever keep before me the
great privilege of being an heir of your glory, and a citizen of heaven.
May my life in its praise and worship of you now be the closest
possible approximation to the praise and worship of heaven.

— **Derek Prime**

*Place me like a seal over your heart, like
a seal on your arm; for love is as strong as death,
its jealousy unyielding as the grave. It burns like
blazing fire, like a mighty flame.*
Song of Songs 8:6

Passage for the Day: Song of Songs 8:6–7

A woman expects every sexual union to bring her closer to her husband and to remain closer to him ever after.... An hour of peaceful togetherness in which the woman knows that her husband is really beside her, an hour during which he really participates in everything she tells him and he tells her, is likely to mean a great deal more to most women than any stormy sexual encounter during which she loves her husband, to be sure, but in which her husband actually gives himself to the experience rather than to his wife.

— Paul Plattner

September 5

Why are you downcast, O my soul?
Why so disturbed within me? Put your hope in God,
for I will yet praise him, my Savior and my God.
Psalm 42:11

Passage for the Day: Psalm 42:5–11

The more you recognize death around you, the sweeter will seem the love of the Lord. You will know him better; you will realize the pragmatic and immediate power of his salvation—for wherever death is, there can also be the manifestation of his glorious victory. And you, child—you may stride with freedom, even *through* the difficulties, grief and the hard road, mourning and bereavement.

— **Walter Wangerin, Jr.**

May 14

*Preach the Word; be prepared in season and out of
season; correct, rebuke and encourage—with great
patience and careful instruction.*
2 Timothy 4:2

Passage for the Day: 2 Timothy 3:14–4:5

Does not our preaching contain too much of our own
opinions and convictions, and too little of Jesus Christ? . . . Let us
try to get away from the poverty and pettiness of our own little
convictions and problems, and seek the wealth and splendor that are
vouchsafed to us in Jesus Christ.

— **Dietrich
Bonhoeffer**

September 4

Keep yourselves in God's love as you wait for the mercy of our Lord Jesus Christ to bring you to eternal life.
Jude 21

Passage for the Day: Jude 20–23

In the love that any intelligent creature feels for God there must always be a measure of mystery. It is even possible that it is almost wholly mystery, and that our attempt to find reasons is merely a rationalizing of a love already mysteriously present in the heart as a result of some secret operation of the Spirit within us.

— A.W. Tozer

May 15

Declare his glory among the nations, his marvelous deeds among all peoples.
1 Chronicles 16:24

Passage for the Day: 1 Chronicles 16:8–36

The real miracle in my life had nothing to do with [a cancer] operation on my [pitching] arm. It had to do with something Jesus Christ had done for me two thousand years before, when he had died for me and made it possible for me to live in fellowship with him.

— **Dave Dravecky**

September 3

He has showed you, O man, what is good. And what does the LORD require of you? To act justly and to love mercy and to walk humbly with your God.
Micah 6:8

Passage for the Day: Micah 6:6–8

Believing as I do that Christ's words to Nicodemus are relevant to the situation of modern man and that we must be "born again" in no way relieves me of my responsibility to pursue social justice, to act in compassion toward my fellowman and to seek a better world. For, while man is a sinner, God has implanted within each of us a conscience, and with it we become responsible for our own actions and chargeable with the responsibility to do mercy, seek justice and walk humbly before our God. We cannot escape the fact that we are our brother's keeper.

— John B. Anderson

"I am the vine; you are the branches. If a man remains in me and I in him, he will bear much fruit; apart from me you can do nothing."
John 15:5

Passage for the Day: John 15:1–8

Authentic, lasting significance is hid with Christ. . . . That is to say, a man cannot find significance in any lasting way apart from Christ. So, if a man is in Christ, and submitted to God's plan and purpose, then he can satisfy his greatest need in a way that endures.

— **Patrick Morley**

September 2

"Here I am! I stand at the door and knock.
If anyone hears my voice and opens the door, I will
come in and eat with him, and he with me."
Revelation 3:20

Passage for the Day: Revelation 3:14–22

    This promise of Christ testifies that any individual conscious of his God-void and rebellion against the will of God can invite him into his life. Christ never forces his way into an individual's life, but responds only when invited. At that moment, the individual is spiritually made alive.

— **Tim LaHaye**

May 17

He and his kind will be put to shame;
craftsmen are nothing but men. Let them all come
together and take their stand; they will be
brought down to terror and infamy.
Isaiah 44:11

Passage for the Day: Isaiah 44:6–11

Idolatry is placing our longings for what only God can provide in the hands of a creature instead of the Creator. When I live for my work, or my wife, then I have made them my false god. When I am failed (and I can be absolutely sure that a false god will be impotent at the point of my greatest need), then I will experience the shame of failure and misplaced trust. The writers of Scripture are crystal clear that dependence on a false god will inevitably result in loss, pain and shame (Isaiah 42:17; 44:9–11). A false god will disappoint.

— **Dan Allender**

September 1

"I will betroth you to me forever; I will betroth you in righteousness and justice, in love and compassion."
Hosea 2:19

Passage for the Day: Hosea 2:16–23

There is something divine in true marriage. It is like a triangle: it takes three to get married—a man, a woman and God. Francis de Sales put it this way, "If the glue is good, two pieces of wood glued together will cleave so fast to each other that they can be more easily broken in any other place than where they were joined. God glues the husband to the wife with his own blood."

— **G.R. Slater**

May 18

*Both the one who makes men holy and those who are
made holy are of the same family. So Jesus is not
ashamed to call them brothers.*
Hebrews 2:11

Passage for the Day: Hebrews 2:5–18

Our approach to the throne of grace (Hebrews 4:16) is not
on the basis of our victories. We are not invited because we are
worthy. Jesus our brother opens up the way for us to come in our
weaknesses, temptations and failures. He is with us in sympathy
and help, not at the end of our struggle, but all the way through.
— **Reuben R. Welch**

August 31

*Dear friend, I pray that you may enjoy good health
and that all may go well with you,
even as your soul is getting along well.*
3 John 2

Passage for the Day: 3 John 1–8

There should be a degree in which you and I look in friendly terms toward the fellowship of believers. And when we do that, we should make a commitment to it. On the basis of the friendly commitment to the fellowship of believers, we should then be giving of ourselves in some ways so that we are building up dear-friend relationships.

— **D. Stuart Briscoe**

May 19

*Elisha turned away and walked back and
forth in the room and then got on the bed
and stretched out upon him once more.
The boy sneezed seven times and opened his eyes.*
2 Kings 4:35

Passage for the Day: 2 Kings 4:32–37

We don't have to explain miracles; all we have to do is
accept them.

— **Ben Carson**

He prayed to the LORD, "O LORD, is this not what I said when I was still at home? That is why I was so quick to flee to Tarshish. I knew that you are a gracious and compassionate God, slow to anger and abounding in love, a God who relents from sending calamity."
Jonah 4:2

Passage for the Day: Jonah 4:1–4

Nothing expresses God's yearning to forgive better than the Book of Jonah. . . . The whole madcap scenario of balky prophet, ocean storm, and whale detour came about because Jonah could not trust God—could not, that is, trust him to be harsh and unrelenting toward Nineveh. As Robert Frost summed up the story, "After Jonah, you could never trust God not to be merciful again."

— **Philip Yancey**

*But Zacchaeus stood up and said to the Lord,
"Look, Lord! Here and now I give half of my possessions
to the poor, and if I have cheated anybody out
of anything, I will pay back four times the amount."
Luke 19:8*

Passage for the Day: Luke 19:1–10

As you read accounts of Jesus working with a great variety of people, courageously talk to Jesus as you would with any human being. Tell him your needs and ask him to bring about in you the same feelings of love and acceptance that you see taking place in the people of the New Testament.

— Jim Conway

August 29

*"To the angel of the church in Sardis write:
These are the words of him who holds the seven spirits of
God and the seven stars. I know your deeds; you have a
reputation of being alive, but you are dead."*
Revelation 3:1

Passage for the Day: Revelation 3:1–6

Cheap grace is the grace we bestow on ourselves. Cheap grace is the preaching of forgiveness without requiring repentance, baptism without church discipline, Communion without confession, absolution without personal confession. Cheap grace is grace without discipleship, grace without the cross, grace without Jesus Christ, living and incarnate.

— **Dietrich Bonhoeffer**

May 21

> *"See, I am doing a new thing! Now it springs up;*
> *do you not perceive it? I am making a way in the*
> *desert and streams in the wasteland."*
> *Isaiah 43:19*

Passage for the Day: Isaiah 43:16–21

Perhaps it's time that Christian men in America check out of the rat race. It's an unwinnable race. Isn't it time we started doing the job we were promoted to when we first trusted in Christ? "Therefore, if anyone is in Christ, he is a new creation; the old has gone, the new has come!" (2 Corinthians 5:17). We are promised a new spiritual nature, but we must be faithful to do our part—to do the new job.

— **Patrick Morley**

August 28

Those living far away fear your wonders;
where morning dawns and evening fades
you call forth songs of joy.
Psalm 65:8

Passage for the Day: Psalm 65:5–13

For a tiny handful of us this is still "My Father's World." We know assuredly that it is he who brought it into being. We are acutely aware that he cares for it deeply. He knows the most minute detail of every bird, flower or tree upon it. They are his. He is theirs. And amid all the lovely interaction between Creator and creation he speaks to me. Therein lies part of his wonder, awe and inspiration.

— **W. Phillip Keller**

May 22

For the grace of God that brings salvation
has appeared to all men.
Titus 2:11

Passage for the Day: Titus 2:11–15

How does one go about praying? I didn't know. I figured if God was God, he would understand if I just told him what was on my mind. I said, "God, I don't know everything about you. I don't think I ever will. But I know I'm a sinner and I know I want to be forgiven. I know I want Christ in my life, and I want to go to heaven. I want to become a Christian. With that, I accept you. Amen."

— **Orel Hershiser**

August 27

This is love for God: to obey his commands.
And his commands are not burdensome.
1 John 5:3

Passage for the Day: 1 John 5:1–5

It is obvious that . . . a God-centered lifestyle cannot be developed and maintained apart from a solid foundation of devotion to God. Only a strong personal relationship with the living God can keep such a commitment from becoming oppressive and legalistic. John writes that God's commands are not burdensome; a godly life is not wearisome, but this is true only because a godly person is first of all devoted to God.

— **Jerry Bridges**

May 23

I know, my God, that you test the heart and are pleased with integrity. All these things I have given willingly and with honest intent.
And now I have seen with joy how willingly your people who are here have given to you.
1 Chronicles 29:17

Passage for the Day: 1 Chronicles 29:14–19

A real man is a man of integrity. That means going all out in everything he does. When he says something, you can count on it, take it to the bank. If I say I'm going to do something, you can consider it done. The first time I violate that, my credibility is shot. Our reputations are only as good as our last performances.

— **Mike Singletary**

August 26

*"The pride of your heart has deceived you,
you who live in the clefts of the rocks and make
your home on the heights, you who say to yourself,
'Who can bring me down to the ground?'"*
Obadiah 3

Passage for the Day: Obadiah 2–7

I have worked out a simple formula for humility.
IF WE RECOGNIZE THAT:
1. God created this universe, including us, and
2. God shows that he is much more powerful than we are by what he does and has done in our world, and
3. God gives each of us abilities that we cannot supply to ourselves or explain our worthiness of,
THEN WE ARE HUMBLED.

— **Ben Carson**

May 24

"But you will receive power when the Holy Spirit comes on you; and you will be my witnesses in Jerusalem, and in all Judea and Samaria, and to the ends of the earth."
Acts 1:8

Passage for the Day: Acts 1:1–8

I tell [these inner-city kids] that I love them with the love of the Lord Jesus Christ who loved them so much that he gave his life for them. I share that nothing in life satisfies like he does. . . I read a few passages of Scripture and then relay to them the plan of salvation. . . . Why do I take time out of my hectic schedule to be with these kids in North Philadelphia? Because God has given me a platform, and if I don't use it, I commit sin. Therefore, I choose to obey my Lord. And I enjoy it.

— **Reggie White**

August 25

*"I am the Living One; I was dead, and
behold I am alive for ever and ever! And I hold the
keys of death and Hades."*
Revelation 1:18

Passage for the Day: Revelation 1:17–20

[While anxiously waiting for biopsy results,] I also thought about my eternal destination. I felt a deep sense of security there—that if I were going to die, I knew what would come next. That meant a lot to me.

I don't ordinarily think much about heaven and hell. I'm too busy keeping up with the day-to-day concerns of life. But in those days I found that my perspective shifted. Some things that mattered a lot in the day-to-day routine of living mattered much less. Some things that I seldom considered mattered a great deal more.

— **Dave Dravecky**

May 25

"Listen to me, O house of Jacob, all you who remain of the house of Israel, you whom I have upheld since you were conceived, and have carried since your birth."
Isaiah 46:3

Passage for the Day: Isaiah 46:1–4

God wants to be loved as a father and mother are loved by their children, as a friend by a friend, as a man by his wife and a wife by her husband, as a sick person by a caring nurse and as a guest by his host. God finds great joy when we express our feelings toward him.

— **Walter Trobisch**

August 24

My soul clings to you;
your right hand upholds me.
Psalm 63:8

Passage for the Day: Psalm 63:1–8

Any simpleton can follow the narrow path in the light: faith's rare wisdom enables us to march on in the dark with infallible accuracy, since she places her hand in that of her great Guide. Between this and heaven there may be rougher weather yet, but it is all provided for by our covenant Head.

— **Charles Spurgeon**

May 26

So that, having been justified by his grace, we might
become heirs having the hope of eternal life.
Titus 3:7

Passage for the Day: Titus 3:1–4

Janice and I entered this difficult period, when life was
often beyond our control, with a deep conviction that God was for us.
Jesus had given his life for us. There was nothing else—no other
good thing—he would withhold. We expected to see God's love in
whatever came—however strange the twists and turns of the road
might be. That fundamental belief gave us a deep well of hope to
draw from.

— **Dave Dravecky**

August 23

Anyone who runs ahead and does not continue in the teaching of Christ does not have God; whoever continues in the teaching has both the Father and the Son.
2 John 9

Passage for the Day: 2 John 8–9

To go beyond the fundamental truths that the church holds dear is to make "gains" that are really losses. We must know the truth, live the truth, defend the truth and share the truth with others. But we must never go *beyond* that truth. . . . This is why God's work is so important, and why it demands the very best that we can give it.

— **David Wiersbe and**
Warren Wiersbe

May 27

Then hear from heaven, your dwelling place.
Forgive, and deal with each man according to
all he does, since you know his heart
(for you alone know the hearts of men).
2 Chronicles 6:30

Passage for the Day: 2 Chronicles 6:28–31

The only thing to depend on in man is what God has done in him. When you come to work for Jesus Christ, always ask yourself, "Do I believe Jesus Christ can do anything for that case?" Am I as confident in his power as he is in his own? If you deal with people without any faith in Jesus Christ it will crush the very life out of you. If we believe in Jesus Christ, we can face every problem the world holds.

— **Oswald Chambers**

August 22

"We have sinned and done wrong.
We have been wicked and have rebelled;
we have turned away from your commands and laws."
Daniel 9:5

Passage for the Day: Daniel 9:4–11

I can only keep trying to be faithful, even though I feel faithless most of the time. What else can I do but keep praying to you, even when I feel dark; to keep writing about you, even when I feel numb; to keep speaking your name, even when I feel alone. Come, Lord Jesus, come. Have mercy on me, a sinner. Amen.

— **Henri Nouwen**

May 28

Love is patient, love is kind. It does not envy,
it does not boast, it is not proud.
1 Corinthians 13:4

Passage for the Day: 1 Corinthians 13:1–13

Marriage is a stage on which real love—the kind the apostle Paul described as the greatest virtue—can be enacted for the world to see: the kind of love that enables us to endure wrong with patience, to resist evil with conviction, to enjoy the good things with gusto, to give richly of ourselves with humility, and to nourish another's soul with long-suffering.

— **Larry Crabb**

August 21

"Blessed are those who mourn,
for they will be comforted."
Matthew 5:4

Passage for the Day: Matthew 5:3–10

When you mourn, when you get to the point of sorrow for your sins, when you admit that you have no other option but to cast all your cares on him, and when there is truly no other name that you can call, then cast all your cares on him, for he is waiting in the midst of the storm.

— **Max Lucado**

May 29

When Jesus landed and saw a large crowd, he had compassion on them and healed their sick.
Matthew 14:14

Passage for the Day: Matthew 14:13–21

The watchword for us all, no matter where God leads us, will be "love." Love is the one quality the world can discern that sets Christians apart and makes Christianity distinct from every other religion. If we fail to act on this truth, we will lose our right to be heard.

— **Thomas Hale**

August 20

*Enoch walked with God; then he was no more,
because God took him away.
Genesis 5:24*

Passage for the Day: Genesis 5:21–24

It is evident [from Genesis 5 and Hebrews 11] . . . that Enoch's life was centered in God: God was the focal point, the polestar of his very existence. . . . This personal attitude toward God is what we call devotion to God. . . . Devotion is not an activity; it is an attitude toward God.

— **Jerry Bridges**

May 30

*They spoke about the God of Jerusalem as they did
about the gods of the other peoples of the
world—the work of men's hands.*
2 Chronicles 32:19

Passage for the Day: 2 Chronicles 32:10–19

The terrible truth is that the gods of this world are no more
worthy of our ultimate trust than are the men who created them.
— **Frederick
Buechner**

August 19

But it is you, a man like myself, my companion,
my close friend.
Psalm 55:13

Passage for the Day: Psalm 55:1–14

Entering friendship involves revealing yourself in confidence to another, and thus becoming vulnerable. This is as it should be, but it is what makes betrayal so evil and faithfulness so virtuous.

— **David W. Smith**

May 31

When they saw the courage of Peter and John and realized that they were unschooled, ordinary men, they were astonished and they took note that these men had been with Jesus.
Acts 4:13

Passage for the Day: Acts 4:8–20

"Who is the God you worship?" I have asked men this question on many occasions. . . . Again and again they stop after a few confused mutterings and admit God is quite unreal. When pinned down they have little to say. Why should a man bother about God if that is all he means to them?

But consider Jesus Christ! . . .

If you want to know what God is like, look at his Son. If you want to hear God, listen to his Son! . . . You can't go wrong trusting Christ, following Christ, worshiping Christ! He will lead you to a personal, dynamic experience of God.

— Richard Halverson

August 18

There is no fear in love. But perfect love drives out fear, because fear has to do with punishment. The one who fears is not made perfect in love.
1 John 4:18

Passage for the Day: 1 John 4:7–21

This world is filled with threats—some imagined, some real—to our safety, to our sense of being okay. The ultimate security, the only true safety, is to be in right relationship with the God who is the alpha and omega, the beginning and the end. He was there before the beginning. He has no end. He has seen and suffered all. He has known our fears. He sets us free.

— **Daniel Taylor**

June 1

The righteous man leads a blameless life;
blessed are his children after him.
Proverbs 20:7

Passage for the Day: Proverbs 20:6–7

It seems the largest mail order seed company in the country decided to go out of business, despite the fact that sales were higher than ever. Unfortunately, so were nonpayments by their mail order sales force. . . . The average age of these delinquent salesmen was ten years! The final straw came when the company attempted to contact the parents, hoping they would help in collection, only to discover that the parents actually encouraged the kids. . . .

It's unfortunate that later these parents probably won't understand why irresponsible children become irresponsible adults.

— **Larry Burkett**

August 17

Now when Daniel learned that the decree had been published, he went home to his upstairs room where the windows opened toward Jerusalem. Three times a day he got down on his knees and prayed, giving thanks to his God, just as he had done before.
Daniel 6:10

Passage for the Day: Daniel 6:10–14

Just as the Christian is not bound to ritual laws that regulate the preparation for prayer, so he is not absolutely bound to set times for prayer. Yet there are times that are more appropriate for prayer than others: the gathering together for worship, the hours before work and bedtime, the time right before meals, when we need to remind ourselves of the goodness of God. But a Christian should feel free to pray anywhere, anytime, in the midst of daily work and play as well as in the solitude of his room in the early morning or late in the evening.

— **Donald Bloesch**

June 2

But solid food is for the mature,
who by constant use have trained themselves
to distinguish good from evil.
Hebrews 5:14

Passage for the Day: Hebrews 5:11–6:3

Practice what you know is right. Too often we focus on doing what we've always done. We don't progress, keep in shape, work out daily. The warning is clear: "Solid food is for the mature, who by constant use have trained themselves to distinguish good from evil. Therefore let us leave the elementary teachings about Christ and go on to maturity" (Hebrews 5:14–6:1).

— **Reggie White**

August 16

"Father, if you are willing, take this cup from me;
yet not my will, but yours be done."
Luke 22:42

Passage for the Day: Luke 22:39–46

If I took Jesus seriously, and truly asked God to let me do
his will in my life, would I be where I am right now?

— Jack Perry

June 3

*I also told them about the gracious hand of my God
upon me and what the king had said to me.
Nehemiah 2:18*

Passage for the Day: Nehemiah 2:11–20

When you check in to work tomorrow morning, say to the Lord, "Here I am, Lord, uniquely gifted with skill, time and energy graciously provided by you. I recognize this. And I believe that you have me where you want me, which means that this particular job that I thought last week was a real bummer is, in actual fact, a high calling, and I am going to live and work today as if that is exactly what it is."

— **D. Stuart Briscoe**

August 15

*Have mercy on me, O God, according to your
unfailing love; according to your great compassion
blot out my transgressions.*
Psalm 51:1

Passage for the Day: Psalm 51:1–17

Repentant people realize that inexcusable wrong can either
be judged or forgiven, never understood and overlooked, and so they
beg for forgiveness with no thought of deserving it. Truly repentant
people are the ones who begin to grasp God's amazing grace, the
ones who know that they need only confess to experience the
forgiveness that is always there in infinite supply.

— **Larry Crabb**

June 4

*Now I want you to realize that the head of every man is
Christ, and the head of the woman is man, and
the head of Christ is God.*
1 Corinthians 11:3

Passage for the Day: 1 Corinthians 11:2–10

Headship means responsibility and initiative: responsibility
to act in love; initiative to act in service. As Christ acted in self-
giving love and self-humbling service (giving us a whole new
meaning to "headship"), so husbands take the initiative in building
an atmosphere of loving, self-sacrificing service.

— **David Augsburger**

August 14

Since everything will be destroyed in this way,
what kind of people ought you to be? You ought to
live holy and godly lives.
2 Peter 3:11

Passage for the Day: 2 Peter 3:11–14

The true saint is not one who has become convinced that he himself is holy, but one who is overwhelmed by the realization that God, and God alone, is holy.

— **Thomas Merton**

June 5

Impress them on your children.
Talk about them when you sit at home
and when you walk along the road,
when you lie down and when you get up.
Deuteronomy 6:7

Passage for the Day: Deuteronomy 6:1–9

To any father who really cares about his children, nothing is of greater importance than their training for discipline, their instruction in principles. Together these make up their *character,* which Aristotle defined as the decisions a person makes when the choice is not obvious.

— **D. Bruce Lockerbie**

August 13

He says, "It is too small a thing for you to be my servant to restore the tribes of Jacob and bring back those of Israel I have kept. I will also make you a light for the Gentiles, that you may bring my salvation to the ends of the earth."
Isaiah 49:6

Passage for the Day: Isaiah 49:1–7

In Luke 2:22–35 we meet Simeon, a man who has grown old waiting for the Messiah—the consolation of Israel. As he takes the infant Jesus into his arms, Simeon sings his praise to God, proclaiming in the words of Isaiah 49:6 that this baby would not only be a light for Israel, but also for the Gentiles.

It was good news to finally be able to embrace the Promised One. But far and away the best news of all is that he embraces us. . . . Deep inside his tired old heart, he knew that the infant he held in his arms was in truth the One who had been holding him all his life long.

— **Michael Card**

June 6

But the Lord said to Ananias, "Go! This man is my chosen instrument to carry my name before the Gentiles and their kings and before the people of Israel."
Acts 9:15

Passage for the Day: Acts 9:1–16

In 2 Corinthians, there's a list as long as a tall man's arm relating all the things Paul endured. He was beaten, imprisoned, and there were many attempts on his life before he was finally killed, beheaded in Rome because of his love for the gospel. And just before the end of his life, he was able to write to Timothy: "I have fought the good fight, I have finished the race, I have kept the faith" (2 Timothy 4:7).

— **Bill McCartney**

August 12

They exchanged the truth of God for a lie, and worshiped and served created things rather than the Creator—who is forever praised. Amen.
Romans 1:25

Passage for the Day: Romans 1:18–25

If Christianity is no more than a system that answers all of life's questions, then to admit any . . . shortcomings is to be something less than a good Christian. But in our own attempts to be good Christians, we undermine our need for God. We want Christianity to work. We want it to exist in a closed system where every question has an answer, every problem has a solution. We want to show the world a neat, clean, open-and-shut case for Christianity. But in the process, we unknowingly shut out God.

Claiming to be wise, we become fools; we exchange the truth of God for a lie.

— **John Fischer**

June 7

*It is the Sovereign L*ORD *who helps me.*
Who is he that will condemn me?
They will all wear out like a garment;
the moths will eat them up.
Isaiah 50:9

Passage for the Day: Isaiah 50:6–9

The Servant of God understood that faith was not a protective shield against the brutality of those who beat him or the ignominy of those who pulled out his beard. In that culture, nothing could have been more shameful than having one's beard plucked. Nevertheless, no one could stand as his accuser and bring his soul to shame because the Father stood as his advocate and judge.

— **Dan Allender**

August 11

*I would like you to be free from concern. An unmarried
man is concerned about the Lord's affairs—how
he can please the Lord.*
1 Corinthians 7:32

Passage for the Day: 1 Corinthians 7:32–38

Is Paul putting down marriage? Not at all. He is simply
holding up another commitment—an even more demanding and
absorbing one: one hundred percent, all-out devotion to God.

— **Leonard LeSourd**

June 8

For this reason Christ is the mediator of a new covenant,
that those who are called may receive the promised
eternal inheritance—now that he has died as
a ransom to set them free from the sins
committed under the first covenant.
Hebrews 9:15

Passage for the Day: Hebrews 9:11–15

Because the Son of God became Man, because he is the
Mediator, for that reason alone the only true relation we can have
with him is to follow him. Discipleship is bound to Christ as the
Mediator, and where it is properly understood, it necessarily implies
faith in the Son of God as the Mediator. Only the Mediator, the God-
Man, can call men to follow him.

— **Dietrich**
Bonhoeffer

***A man who has riches without understanding is
like the beasts that perish.
Psalm 49:20***

Passage for the Day: Psalm 49:16–20

In this life the wealthy often inspire awe, admiration and praise. But this adulation will be short-lived. The possessions that are the basis of their pride and self-aggrandizement will not survive past the grave. Verse 20 describes the final state of the man who leaves God out of his life. Without understanding, he is like the beasts that perish. His power, influence and wealth won't carry any weight in eternity.

Lord, may I learn to live always, not for this life only, but with "eternity's values in view."

— **Don Wyrtzen**

June 9

*My son, keep your father's commands and
do not forsake your mother's teaching.*
Proverbs 6:20

Passage for the Day: Proverbs 6:20–29

God *does not* give us men—he gives us *boys.* To us, as
parents, he gives the task of forging these boys into men. To help
equip us for the task, God has provided the book of Proverbs, which
is largely the advice of a father to his son. . . . Our children are our
legacy. As a parent, are you taking that thought seriously?

— **Charles Swindoll**

August 9

If we confess our sins, he is faithful and just and will forgive us our sins and purify us from all unrighteousness.
1 John 1:9

Passage for the Day: 1 John 1:5–10

To mourn for your sins is a natural outflow of poverty of spirit. The second beatitude [Blessed are those who mourn] should follow the first [Blessed are the poor in spirit]. But that's not always the case. Many deny their weakness. Many know they are wrong, yet pretend they are right. As a result, they never taste the exquisite sorrow of repentance.

Of all the paths to joy, this one has to be the strangest. True blessedness, Jesus says, begins with deep sadness.

— **Max Lucado**

June 10

*"What has happened to us is a result of our evil deeds
and our great guilt, and yet, our God, you have
punished us less than our sins have deserved and
have given us a remnant like this."*
Ezra 9:13

Passage for the Day: Ezra 9:6,13–15

Just like I do with teammates, I want to be able to sit with
my kids and tell them some of the things I have done. Not to glorify
sin. Not to justify it. Not to say everybody does it so it must be okay.
Rather, because I'm not proud of it and because I don't want them to
feel unique. Most of all, I want them to know that by the grace of
God, he brought me through it and out of it, and he can do the same
for them.

— **Mike Singletary**

August 8

"Therefore I say to them,
'This is what the Sovereign LORD says: None of my words
will be delayed any longer; whatever I say will be
fulfilled, declares the Sovereign LORD.'"
Ezekiel 12:28

Passage for the Day: Ezekiel 12:21–28

We need time to know God, and he has given it to us. Hebrews refers to God's time as Today: "Today, if you hear his voice, do not harden your hearts" (Hebrews 4:7). Today is always a day of opportunity. Hebrews urges us to enter God's rest Today. God's rest I take to be the state in which everything else stops and we have the opportunity we need to know God.

— **Tim Stafford**

*"The fig tree forms its early fruit; the blossoming vines
spread their fragrance. Arise, come, my darling;
my beautiful one, come with me."*
Song of Songs 2:13

Passage for the Day: Song of Songs 2:3–13

No one can make a claim to faithfulness in marriage if he does not keep the door open to the possibilities that his relationship can be better tomorrow than it is today.

— **Lewis B. Smedes**

August 7

*Do you not know that your body is a temple
of the Holy Spirit, who is in you, whom you have
received from God? You are not your own.*
1 Corinthians 6:19

Passage for the Day: 1 Corinthians 6:18–20

We belong entirely to Christ. His Spirit has taken
possession of us at baptism. We are the temples of the Holy Spirit.
Our thoughts, our actions, our desires, are by rights more his than
our own. But we have to struggle to ensure that God always receives
from us what we owe him by right.

— **Thomas Merton**

June 12

Now it is required that those
who have been given a trust
must prove faithful.
1 Corinthians 4:2

Passage for the Day: 1 Corinthians 4:1–5

A boy who has a father who is committed to his mother will
have a tremendous advantage when he becomes a husband. He will
have an intuitive understanding that his commitment in marriage is
not a right to be happy, but to demonstrate a willingness to be
responsible. Even when it's inconvenient. Even when it crowds out
his personal happiness.

— Steve Farrar

August 6

*Refrain from anger and turn from wrath;
do not fret—it leads only to evil.*
Psalm 37:8

Passage for the Day: Psalm 37:1–11

It has been my observation, in counseling on problems of
anger control, that each person who has sought God's help in the
understanding and resolution of his or her anger has, without
exception, received that help. These people have described the
results as "miraculous." There is, indeed, a miracle involved. It is
the miracle of God's love for us, the miracle of his redemptive grace.
— **Richard P. Walters**

June 13

"All the prophets testify about him that everyone who believes in him receives forgiveness of sins through his name."
Acts 10:43

Passage for the Day: Acts 10:34–43

God's gift of forgiveness must be appropriated: that is, it must be accepted on an individual basis. Although it is a universal offer, it has no effect on the sin debt of a man or a woman who has not personally put trust in Christ. It is like a paycheck that is never picked up; it is like a gift certificate that is not redeemed; it is like a lifeline that is ignored by a drowning person.

— Charles Stanley

August 5

*And we have the word of the prophets made more
certain, and you will do well to pay attention to it, as to
a light shining in a dark place, until the day dawns and
the morning star rises in your hearts.*
2 Peter 1:19

Passage for the Day: 2 Peter 1:16–21

God will not reject the world but continues his mysterious
and relentless pursuit of it to the end of time. That is what he is
doing by choosing Israel to be his special people. That is what he is
doing through all the passion and poetry and invective of the
prophets. That is why history plays such a crucial part in the Old
Testament—all those kings and renegades and battles and
invasions and apostasies—because it was precisely through people
like that and events like those that God was at work.

**— Frederick
Buechner**

June 14

Do not merely listen to the word,
and so deceive yourselves. Do what it says.
James 1:22

Passage for the Day: James 1:19–15

Your wisdom in controlling your youngster is one of the best measures of how much you really love and value her. . . . She knows that her mother should have a hand in controlling her too; but you, her father, have an equal share in the job. Your personal examples are very important, too, along with your rules. You won't be able to sell her any double standards on the important issues in life. She will come much closer to following what you do and what you believe than what you say about these issues.

— **John E. Crawford**

August 4

*Let us examine our ways and test them, and
let us return to the LORD.
Lamentations 3:40*

Passage for the Day: Lamentations 3:40–42

As a lawyer or accountant is no better than the effort he
puts into keeping up with his profession, so is the Christian no
better than the effort he puts into self-examination of life's big
questions.

— **Patrick Morley**

June 15

Let us draw near to God with a sincere heart in full assurance of faith, having our hearts sprinkled to cleanse us from a guilty conscience and having our bodies washed with pure water.
Hebrews 10:22

Passage for the Day: Hebrews 10:19–25

You cannot be a complete human being without filling the spiritual void that is inside every person. Training camp Christians [those who attempt to barter with God to achieve success] try to fill that void with religion, money, success, sex, drugs, and the list could go on and on. This void can only be filled with a relationship and continued walking with God through his Son, Jesus Christ.

— **Reggie White**

August 3

If we live, we live to the Lord;
and if we die, we die to the Lord.
So, whether we live or die, we belong to the Lord.
Romans 14:8

Passage for the Day: Romans 14:5–8

Pain and despair are threads that run through us as we move through our journey of bereavement. . . . When we confront our pain and despair and begin to accept the loss, surrendering ourselves to God in our powerlessness, then pain and despair can give way to hope. The unwanted pain can be accepted and transformed. When we accept our pain as our own, suffering can grow into compassion. It's as if the heart opens, and out of sorrow come warmth and joy.

— **Philip W. Williams**

June 16

The LORD answered, "I will be with you,
and you will strike down
all the Midianites together."
Judges 6:16

Passage for the Day: Judges 6:11–24

To a generation of men failed by their fathers and lost in a cloud of confusion, God says, "Don't spend a lifetime in aimless drifting. Don't succumb to mindless misinterpretations of masculine identity. Enter into relationship with me, through Jesus Christ, and allow *me* to lead you into authentic manhood. Become my adopted sons and let me 're-father' you."

— **Bill Hybels**

August 2

The earth is the LORD's, and everything in it,
the world, and all who live in it.
Psalm 24:1

Passage for the Day: Psalm 24:1–10

The Lord didn't create the earth and then abandon it. He is intimately involved with sustaining it. He watches over what belongs to him. My Lord doesn't like loose ends! He not only sustains his creation; he watches over me too and allows me to reflect his creativity!

I praise you, Lord, for your incredible imagination and creativity. I thank you that I can, in a very small way, imitate it.

— **Don Wyrtzen**

June 17

*Through him everyone who believes
is justified from everything you could not
be justified from by the law of Moses.*
Acts 13:39

Passage for the Day: Acts 13:38–41

I've always been a wholehearted guy, and I've always
wanted a full measure of whatever was out there. I've never wanted
just part of the package, part of the prize. I want it all! . . . I knew I
wanted a deeper walk with the Lord. And that day, I realized what I
had been missing—I hadn't been born again!

I wanted more. I wanted all of it. Right then and there, I
prayed hard to receive the full measure of God's love. It was the
most exciting moment of my life!

— **Bill McCartney**

August 1

Simon Peter, a servant and apostle of Jesus Christ,
To those who through the righteousness of our God and
Savior Jesus Christ have received a faith as
precious as ours . . .
2 Peter 1:1

Passage for the Day: 2 Peter 1:1–2

We have come [to Nepal] because God has given us a love for the people, especially for those suffering in body and spirit. This love does not arise from ourselves—it is a gift purely from God. Out of that love has grown a desire to introduce others to the person who has meant more to us than any other: Jesus Christ. To neglect sharing with our Nepali friends the joy of knowing him would make a pretense of our friendship. To withhold from them this greatest gift would be to no longer love them.

— **Thomas Hale**

June 18

You have stolen my heart, my sister, my bride;
you have stolen my heart with one glance of your eyes,
with one jewel of your necklace.
Song of Songs 4:9

Passage for the Day: Song of Songs 4:8–15

Sometimes I look at Sandy sleeping, unaware of me, vulnerable as a child, and remember that she lived a good part of her life before I even entered it. The face of a sleeping woman, of *this* sleeping woman, is profound. With its soft lines, with its hidden eyes, with its closed lips, it says: "Eleven years are barely enough to get beneath the skin—let alone to the heart—of the mystery that is a woman."

This woman is my wife. But she is also a sweet stranger, beyond the knowing of a lifetime. She surprises me, and I am glad for that because it renews our marriage.

— Rodney Clapp

July 31

The LORD is good to those whose hope is in him,
to the one who seeks him.
Lamentations 3:25

Passage for the Day: Lamentations 3:19–27

Our heavenly Father desires to have fellowship with each of us. He desires that while we were still sinners, still separated by the debt of sin. Paul writes, "But God demonstrates his own love for us in this: While we were still sinners, Christ died for us" (Romans 5:8). Until all aspects of this verse sink deep into our emotional being, we will never be free of the feelings of condemnation that accompany sin. The strategy that secured our forgiveness was God's idea: he initiated it. He wants us for his very own.

— **Charles Stanley**

June 19

Train a child in the way he should go, and
when he is old he will not turn from it.
Proverbs 22:6

Passage for the Day: Proverbs 22:4–6

The verse doesn't mean "train up a child as you see him." Rather, "if you want your training to be meaningful and wise, be observant and discover your child's way, and adapt your training accordingly.". . . In Proverbs 22:6, the word *way* is used in [this] sense: "train up a child in keeping with his characteristics." And his characteristics are distinct and set. There is a bent already established within every child God places in our care.

— Charles Swindoll

July 30

Does not the potter have the right to make out of the same lump of clay some pottery for noble purposes and some for common use?
Romans 9:21

Passage for the Day: Romans 9:16–21

God molds us and makes us and holds us in his hand. No matter what happens in this life, I'm in his hand. What a mighty God we serve! Right or wrong, up or down, poverty or wealth, sickness or health, come what may, I am in his hand. Hallelujah, I am in his hand.

— **H. Beecher Hicks**

June 20

*"Is not this the kind of fasting I have chosen:
to loose the chains of injustice and untie the cords of the
yoke, to set the oppressed free and break every yoke?"*
Isaiah 58:6

Passage for the Day: Isaiah 58:6–12

The average American today suffers no twinge of conscience when he passes the sick man on the road. He knows he has paid the "Good Samaritan" to come along after him and take care of this rather unpleasant social obligation. But the import of Christ's teaching is very plain. He expects us to take the role of the Good Samaritan, and not delegate our Christian love and compassion and concern in every instance to a paid professional or functionary. We are enjoined to love our neighbor—not just to pay taxes to employ someone else to love our neighbor.

— **John B. Anderson**

July 29

"In those days, at that time," declares the L*ord*, *"search will be made for Israel's guilt, but there will be none, and for the sins of Judah, but none will be found, for I will forgive the remnant I spare."*
Jeremiah 50:20

Passage for the Day: Jeremiah 50:18–20

As a Christian I believe my past is forgiven; I can start over with a clean slate. The mistakes of the past need not hold me back. Neither does my fear of failure—because as a Christian I believe God is in ultimate control of my life.

— **Tom Landry**

June 21

*Therefore, since we are receiving a kingdom that cannot
be shaken, let us be thankful, and so worship God
acceptably with reverence and awe.*
Hebrews 12:28

Passage for the Day: Hebrews 12:18–29

In our day we must begin to recover a sense of awe and
profound reverence for God. We must begin to view him once again
in the infinite majesty that alone belongs to him who is the Creator
and Supreme Ruler of the entire universe.

— **Jerry Bridges**

July 28

*But you, O God, do see trouble and grief; you consider it
to take it in hand. The victim commits himself to you;
you are the helper of the fatherless.*
Psalm 10:14

Passage for the Day: Psalm 10:12–18

As I sat there listening to [the orphan] Krishna, . . . the
verse [James 1:27] began to take on new meaning for me. It meant
that if I were not ready to care for orphans in their distress, then
there was something very wrong with my religion. Not being content
with my exegesis of this verse, God seemed further to be asking me,
"If you are not ready to care for *this* orphan in his distress, who are
you ever going to care for?"

That day, Krishna did not return to his village.

— **Thomas Hale**

June 22

When word came to Sanballat, Tobiah, Geshem the Arab and the rest of our enemies that I had rebuilt the wall and not a gap was left in it—though up to that time I had not set the doors in the gates . . .
Nehemiah 6:1

Passage for the Day: Nehemiah 6:1–4

My friends, consider the wall. . . . A bearing wall is a wall you cannot do without. . . . But it cannot be a bearing wall unless it is inextricably, fundamentally connected to the foundation. Now, if the wall that is around your life is not connected to the foundation, it is not a bearing wall. If the walls around your life are not connected to the rock, it will not sustain the weight of your problems, your difficulties, your trials . . . You need to be connected to the rock. "For no one can lay any foundation other than the one already laid, which is Jesus Christ" (1 Corinthians 3:11).

— H. Beecher Hicks

July 27

Be self-controlled and alert. Your enemy the
devil prowls around like a roaring lion looking for
someone to devour.
1 Peter 5:8

Passage for the Day: 1 Peter 5:8–9

The enemy is no fool. He has a strategically designed game plan, a diabolical method he employs time and time again. When he wants to destroy a family, he focuses on the man. For if he can neutralize the man . . . he has neutralized the family. And the damage that takes place when a man's family leadership is neutralized is beyond calculation.

— **Steve Farrar**

June 23

He did what was right in the eyes of the LORD,
just as his father David had done.
2 Kings 18:3

Passage for the Day: 2 Kings 18:1–8

Two things . . . every father must learn in determining to set a wholesome example for his children. First, a father must humble himself and admit that he can't be the ultimate and faultless example; he can only serve to reflect the image of a higher Example for his sons and daughters to follow. Second, a father must be quick to acknowledge when he has been wrong, and then seek his children's forgiveness. This may be a father's highest example of Christian virtue; it may also be the hardest for him to attain.

— **D. Bruce Lockerbie**

July 26

The LORD is good, a refuge in times of trouble.
He cares for those who trust in him.
Nahum 1:7

Passage for the Day: Nahum 1:7–15

Everyone has noticed how hard it is to turn our thoughts to God when everything is going well with us. We "have all we want" is a terrible saying when "all" does not include God. We find God an interruption. As Saint Augustine says somewhere, "God wants to give us something, but cannot, because our hands are full—there's nowhere for him to put it."

— C.S. Lewis

June 24

Now the Bereans were of more noble character than the Thessalonians, for they received the message with great eagerness and examined the Scriptures every day to see if what Paul said was true.
Acts 17:11

Passage for the Day: Acts 17:10–15

Most of our character is established early in life. Adversity can help build it. Coaches can help mold it. But in our adult years, the only thing I've seen that can radically change a person's basic character is a relationship with Jesus Christ.

— **Tom Landry**

July 25

*"Who is this that darkens my counsel with
words without knowledge?"*
Job 38:2

Passage for the Day: Job 38:1–33

Sometimes God answers us with questions—questions that leave us humbled, awed, speechless, weak and believing—believing not because we've found the answer, but because we've seen God. It doesn't matter that we have more questions now than when we started. It matters that we see God, for in the seeing, we discover that the truest answer to all our questions is to worship him.

— **John Fischer**

June 25

Like cattle that go down to the plain, they were given rest by the Spirit of the LORD. This is how you guided your people to make for yourself a glorious name.
Isaiah 63:14

Passage for the Day: Isaiah 63:11–14

Too much stress—especially stress that is not relieved by times of rest and renewal—can harm us physically, mentally and spiritually. . . . Christians must wake up to the fact that they are burning themselves out just as quickly as everyone else is! Change is occurring so rapidly and hurry sickness is so rampant in our society that avoiding stress damage takes an extra effort. And the sad fact is that relatively few people—even Christians—are making that extra effort.

— **Archibald Hart**

July 24

Husbands, in the same way be considerate as you live
with your wives, and treat them with respect as the
weaker partner and as heirs with you of the gracious
gift of life, so that nothing will hinder your prayers.
1 Peter 3:7

Passage for the Day: 1 Peter 3:1–7

Husbands, do you look at your wives from Peter's
perspective? Are you as concerned about their spiritual fulfillment
as you are about your own? Do you treat them with genuine respect?

— **D. Stuart Briscoe**

June 26

He must manage his own family well and see that his children obey him with proper respect.
1 Timothy 3:4

Passage for the Day: 1 Timothy 3:1–7

[The] spirit of rebellion has come about because children have never learned respect for authority as their parents did not exercise authority; on the other hand, it is also possible that they did not learn respect for authority because the parents misused it. Both are equally dangerous. It is no wonder that there are so many pitfalls in the exercising of authority: he who wields authority wields a God-given weapon, and he must constantly be on guard lest he misuse it for selfish ends. Authority must never be exercised in an arbitrary, unreasonable manner.

— J.H. Waterink

July 23

So I bought the field at Anathoth from my cousin
Hanamel and weighed out for him
seventeen shekels of silver.
Jeremiah 32:9

Passage for the Day: Jeremiah 32:6–29

Buying that field in Anathoth was a deliberate act of hope. All acts of hope expose themselves to ridicule because they seem impractical, failing to conform to visible reality. But in fact they are the reality that is being constructed but is not yet visible. Hope commits us to actions that connect with God's promises.

— Eugene H. Peterson

June 27

So we say with confidence, "The Lord is my helper,
I will not be afraid. What can man do to me?"
Hebrews 13:6

Passage for the Day: Hebrews 13:5–8

Growing up, I had always been at the center of attention. That was exactly how I wanted it. My performance had been for me . . . I had to be the star.

That kind of motivation can keep you going strong, so long as you succeed. But it's not so good for dealing with failure, or with forces beyond your control. Seeing Jesus Christ as your audience shifted the pressure off yourself. You did your best to bring glory to God, not yourself. If you lost, the loss would hurt, but it wouldn't change anything fundamental. God would still be there.

— **Dave Dravecky**

July 22

Now if we are children, then we are heirs—heirs of God and co-heirs with Christ, if indeed we share in his sufferings in order that we may also share in his glory.
Romans 8:17

Passage for the Day: Romans 8:12–17

The love of God has no meaning apart from Calvary. And Calvary has no meaning apart from the holy and just wrath of God. Jesus did not die just to give us peace and a purpose in life; he died to save us from the wrath of God. . . . He died to ransom us from the penalty of sin—the punishment of everlasting destruction, shut out from the presence of the Lord. He died that we, the just objects of God's wrath, should become, by his grace, heirs of God and co-heirs with him.

— **Jerry Bridges**

*"For if you remain silent at this time,
relief and deliverance for the Jews will arise from
another place, but you and your father's family will
perish. And who knows but that you have come to
royal position for such a time as this?"*
Esther 4:14

Passage for the Day: Esther 4:1–17

Though God is invisible, he is invincible. That is the
message of the Book of Esther. The invisible God who may appear to
be absent is the invincible God who is working out his best plan.

That is not only true for a young woman and her people in
ancient Persia; that's true for us today in the twentieth century.

— **Charles Swindoll**

July 21

*"I made a covenant with my eyes
not to look lustfully at a girl."
Job 31:1*

Passage for the Day: Job 31:1–12

Job's point is simply this: There is a difference between a look and a *lustful* look. . . . A one-woman kind of man is a man who demonstrates his commitment by disciplining his eyes.

— **Steve Farrar**

June 29

*However, I consider my life worth nothing to me,
if only I may finish the race and complete the task
the Lord Jesus has given me—the task of
testifying to the gospel of God's grace.
Acts 20:24*

Passage for the Day: Acts 20:17–24

The way in which we measure our standard of living
indicates the race we have decided to run. The American Christian
faces a true dilemma. We can choose the rat race, or we can choose
to not love this world and "throw off everything that hinders and the
sin that so easily entangles, and . . . run with perseverance the race
marked out for us" (Hebrews 12:1).

— **Patrick Morley**

July 20

*Therefore, rid yourselves of all malice and all deceit,
hypocrisy, envy, and slander of every kind.*
1 Peter 2:1

Passage for the Day: 1 Peter 1:22–2:3

Are we going to disbelieve because of the hypocrisy we see
in others or because God won't allow that same hypocrisy in us?
— **Mark Ritchie**

June 30

"Before I formed you in the womb I knew you,
before you were born I set you apart;
I appointed you as a prophet to the nations."
Jeremiah 1:5

Passage for the Day: Jeremiah 1:4–8

If one of your children "surprised" you, let it be the best-kept secret in town. There are no surprises from God's point of view. . . . What may appear to be a surprise to man is always within the sovereign plan of God. . . .

What kind of message are you sending to your children? If in fact they are gifts from God, do they know that? How do your children perceive themselves in the context of your life? Do they see themselves as burdens or blessings? How they answer this last question will pretty much determine whether or not you can keep them on your team.

— **Charles Stanley**

July 19

The LORD appeared to us in the past, saying:
"I have loved you with an everlasting love; I have
drawn you with loving-kindness."
Jeremiah 31:3

Passage for the Day: Jeremiah 31:1–6

I have . . . experienced God's help in many crises. I have
come to realize that God does not want to punish us but, rather, to
fulfill our lives. God created us, loves us, and wants to help us
realize our potential so that we can be useful to others.

— **Ben Carson**

July 1

Consider it pure joy, my brothers,
whenever you face trials of many kinds.
James 1:2

Passage for the Day: James 1:2–8

The better we are at seeing through trials to what they can produce in our lives and our children's lives, the better able we'll be to provide calmness, assurance and genuine love to our children, even in the midst of trying times.

— **Gary Smalley and**
John Trent

July 18

*Command them to do good, to be rich in good deeds, and
to be generous and willing to share.*
1 Timothy 6:18

Passage for the Day: 1 Timothy 6:17–19

God is deeply concerned to see us meet [the poor's] . . .
needs. His concern does not arise because the poor are inherently
better but because they are needy. And from the beginning of
creation, he has desired to meet human needs. He wants to meet
some of them through you and me.

— **Doug Sherman and
William Hendricks**

July 2

"I have no peace, no quietness;
I have no rest, but only turmoil."
Job 3:26

Passage for the Day: Job 3:11–26

Worrying magnifies actual threats and creates imagined ones—both of which trigger the stress response. And because [unlike the story of Job] they *are* imagined or blown out of proportion, these threats cannot be confronted and resolved. . . . It is these more subtle threats that produce the greatest amount of stress damage. Things that worry us, prod us, scare or frighten us—when there is nothing we can do about them—can be the most destructive of all. Perhaps this is why Jesus . . . told us, "Do not let your hearts be troubled and do not be afraid" (John 14:27).

— Archibald Hart

July 17

"Submit to God and be at peace with him;
in this way prosperity will come to you."
Job 22:21

Passage for the Day: Job 22:21–30

Someone once described the contrast between a good life and a godly life as the difference between the top of the ocean and the bottom. On the top, sometimes it's like glass—serene and calm—and other times it's raging and stormy. But hundreds of fathoms below, it is beautiful and consistent, always calm, always peaceful.
— **Bill McCartney**

*"And now what are you waiting for?
Get up, be baptized and wash
your sins away, calling on his name."*
Acts 22:16

Passage for the Day: Acts 22:12–21

He didn't have to be told twice. The legalist Saul was buried, and the liberator Paul was born. He was never the same afterwards. And neither was the world. . . .

Paul never took a course in missions. He never sat in on a committee meeting. He never read a book on church growth. He was just inspired by the Holy Spirit and punch-drunk on the love that makes the impossible possible: salvation.

— **Max Lucado**

July 16

*But just as he who called you is holy, so
be holy in all you do.*
1 Peter 1:15

Passage for the Day: 1 Peter 1:13–16

Let us not . . . delude ourselves with easy and infantile
conceptions of holiness. . . . Mere external respectability, without
deeper or more positive moral values, brings discredit upon the
Christian faith.

— **Thomas Merton**

July 4

> *"I looked for a man among them who would build up the wall and stand before me in the gap on behalf of the land so I would not have to destroy it, but I found none."*
> *Ezekiel 22:30*

Passage for the Day: Ezekiel 22:23–31

In this desperately crucial, convulsive time, *unavailability is a terrible sin.* The times demand big men. Not men who are big shots (they're useless), but men who are big in heart and mind. Great men! Large-souled men!

Men with a vision—whose feet are on the ground but whose eyes are on the far horizon. Farsighted, selfless men. *Men with a goal!* Men whose hearts God has touched. Men committed—*dedicated to God* and his holy, high purposes! Men of integrity!

— **Richard Halverson**

July 15

"Build houses and settle down;
plant gardens and eat what they produce."
Jeremiah 29:5

Passage for the Day: Jeremiah 29:4–14

All of us are given moments, days, months, years of exile. What will we do with them? Wish we were someplace else? Complain? Escape into fantasies? Drug ourselves into oblivion? Or build and plant and marry and seek the shalom of the place we inhabit and the people we are with? Exile reveals what really matters and frees us to pursue what really matters, which is to seek the Lord with all our hearts.

— **Eugene H. Peterson**

July 5

But if you show favoritism,
you sin and are convicted by the law as lawbreakers.
James 2:9

Passage for the Day: James 2:1–11

[God] had endowed every person in the Body with the same capacity to respond to him. In Christ's Body, a teacher of three-year-olds has the same value as a bishop, and that teacher's work may be just as significant. A widow's dollar can equal a millionaire's annuity. Shyness, beauty, eloquence, race, sophistication—none of these matter, only loyalty to the Head, and through the Head to each other.

— Paul Brand

God presented him as a sacrifice of atonement, through faith in his blood. He did this to demonstrate his justice, because in his forbearance he had left the sins committed beforehand unpunished.
Romans 3:25

Passage for the Day: Romans 3:21–26

We believe that the death of Christ is just that point in history at which something absolutely unimaginable from outside shows through into our own world. And if we cannot picture even the atoms of which our own world is built, of course we are not going to be able to picture this. Indeed, if we found that we could fully understand it, that very fact would show it was not what it professes to be—the inconceivable, the uncreated, the thing from beyond nature, striking down into nature like lightning.

— **C.S. Lewis**

July 6

*"As the heavens are higher than the earth,
so are my ways higher than your ways and
my thoughts than your thoughts."*
Isaiah 55:9

Passage for the Day: Isaiah 55:8–13

We seem to be very unwilling to wait for God's timing and
for God's method to meet our needs and our desires. We prefer to
have it done our way, on our timing. . . . Invariably, God's method of
meeting my needs and desires is different from my method.

— Ron Blue

July 13

Though he slay me, yet will I hope in him;
I will surely defend my ways to his face.
Job 13:15

Passage for the Day: Job 13:13–19

True faith depends not upon mysterious signs, celestial fireworks, or grandiose dispensations from a God who is seen as a rich, benevolent uncle; true faith, as Job understood, rests on the assurance that *God is who he is.* Indeed, on that we must be willing to stake our very lives.

— **Charles Colson**

July 7

"My people have committed two sins:
They have forsaken me, the spring of living water,
and have dug their own cisterns,
broken cisterns that cannot hold water."
Jeremiah 2:13

Passage for the Day: Jeremiah 2:9–19

D.L. Moody said about the Bible, "This Book will keep you from sin, or sin will keep you from this Book." Jeremiah knew that too. When people neglected God's Word, when they stopped drinking from the stream of living water, they started digging their own cisterns in the sand.

— **William Petersen**

July 12

Therefore confess your sins to each other and pray for each other so that you may be healed. The prayer of a righteous man is powerful and effective.
James 5:16

Passage for the Day: James 5:13–20

A man who doesn't have at least one other man to whom he can be accountable regarding his failures, hurts and temptations is a prime target for masculine anger.

— Stephen Arterburn and David Stoop

July 8

But the wisdom that comes from heaven is first of all pure; then peace-loving, considerate, submissive, full of mercy and good fruit, impartial and sincere.
James 3:17

Passage for the Day: James 3:13–18

Self-centeredness is the killer. In every bad relationship, it is the deadliest culprit. Poor communication, temper problems, unhealthy responses to dysfunctional family backgrounds, codependent relationships, and personal incompatibility—everything (unless medically caused) flows out of the cesspool of self-centeredness.

— **Larry Crabb**

July 11

This is what the LORD says: "Let not the wise man boast of his wisdom or the strong man boast of his strength or the rich man boast of his riches."
Jeremiah 9:23

Passage for the Day: Jeremiah 9:23–24

We all get caught up in the externals of life, whether it's tennis or golf or business deals, and we run the risk of losing the things most important to us: our own kids.

— Joe Gibbs

July 9

As I have observed, those who plow evil and those who sow trouble reap it.
Job 4:8

Passage for the Day: Job 4:7–8

These pseudo-friends [of Job's], with their criticism and self-righteousness, failed to look at Job's pain from a different point of view. They reached the easy but wrong conclusion that God must be punishing Job for some unrevealed sin.

If we had to choose a friendship like that between David and Jonathan [1 Samuel 18:1] or that of Job and his crew, we would all prefer the kindness and commitment that existed between David and Jonathan. But close friendships don't just happen. They result from the application of principles recorded throughout the Word of God.

— **David W. Smith**

July 10

Or do you show contempt for the riches of his kindness, tolerance and patience, not realizing that God's kindness leads you toward repentance?
Romans 2:4

Passage for the Day: Romans 2:1–4

God seems in no hurry to judge. For now, it appears we can live self-centeredly and not pay a price.

But we can interpret God's delay in *two* ways: either our sin doesn't really offend him a great deal or "... he is patient with [us], not wanting anyone to perish, but everyone to come to repentance" (2 Peter 3:9).

— Larry Crabb